MIRIE'S MAGNIFICENT LOVING LIFE

ONE HEART, TWO HANDS, NINE LIVES

MIRIAM SAMUEL TURNS 90

90 YEARS
1080 MONTHS
32,850 DAYS
788,400 HOURS
A WONDERFUL FAMILY
AMAZING FRIENDS
SPECIAL MEMORIES
A BLESSED LIFE

Happy Birthday

MIRIAM SAMUEL

12.05.24

FOREWORD
By Derede Whitlock

Decoding the Recipe of Life

In a society that often overlooks the invaluable benefits of ageing, Miriam Samuel shares how the fruits of her long life and vast achievements have borne seeds of wisdom over her 90 years of life. This veteran educator and "seniorpreneur", believes that ageing is a privilege and society does not place enough importance on the achievements of its elders, especially women. Balancing their careers, raising children, and running the household, women are bastions of resilience and major assets to society, particularly when it comes to creativity, relationship-building, and leadership abilities.

Born during the Great Depression, Miriam Samuel, affectionately known as "Mirie," was raised with little resources, and limited economic and educational opportunities. She is part of a generation of inspired competitors: individuals with a "work as hard as you can, then work even harder" mindset.

Accepting necessity as the "mother of invention", Mirie always finds creative ways to supplement her income as a way to mitigate the "scarcity mindset" that is common among many Baby Boomers. Most in her generation look forward to retiring comfortably at age 65 with pension and social security benefits, but Mirie has refused to slow down. She has shown that growing older simply means gaining confidence and learning from the life lessons that you only get from a long career and a fulfilling life.

Mirie makes us rethink the potential role that mature women can play in shaping our society. From her childhood adventure, sailing from Anguilla to Antigua one year before the start of World War II, to surviving the COVID 19 pandemic more than 80 years later, Miriam has been blessed with good health, prosperity, peace, and abundance.

From humble beginnings, her parents toiled on several estates throughout Antigua to provide for their eight children. They carved out a path of survival by relying on the land. Although they were labourers and not land owners, the Fleming family's love for farming and their strong connection to the soil were key elements to their survival in the post World War II era.

As the eldest girl in her family, Mirie became the "pseudo-Mom" and caretaker for her siblings. By the time she was 8 years old, she was cooking most of the family's meals and feeding her siblings daily was her responsibility. Her younger sister Inger recalls how she would find creative ways to "stretch the food." If she cooked rice and peas one day, Mirie would cook the rice with spinach the next day and salted fish or meat later that week. The same applied to corn meal or flour. Mirie had many creative recipes.

She also had her own backyard garden to ensure that she always had a choice of ingredients to make a variety of tasty meals. Cooking became her passion — an art form which allowed her "to create much from little." In the process, she brought happiness and relief to her siblings, when many families faced hunger.

Cooking is an integral part of her magical recipe for life. She uses it as a way to bring people together, share stories and create memories. It is a joyful, creative way for her to connect with others, and spread kindness, unity, and love.

As wife to a veteran politician, Miriam exemplified the saying "beside every great man is a great woman." She shared the joys and challenges of maintaining a humble life in the spotlight, during her husband's 32-year political career. Moreover, when she became a widow at age 73 she had to step into the role as head of household, after 45 years of marriage. Paying bills and managing the family finances are tasks that she had to learn as a senior citizen. In essence, she had to step out of her comfort zone and into the driver seat, at a time when many expected her to slow down.

A 40-year educator, Teacher Mirie has impacted hundreds of young minds in ten different schools, thereby touching lives in every parish in Antigua. Throughout her teaching career, she always had a side hustle, but she also had dreams of starting her own full-time business upon retirement. Her passion, expertise and experience provided the tools for her journey as an entrepreneur. She sees her age as an asset and not a drawback, and her wisdom as potential wealth waiting to be packaged and distributed and not just a life experience.

"At the age of 90, you are confident that you don't need to prove anything. Before retiring, I established a market and a customer following, so I was ready to take that leap in starting my business. But it was still a learning process and I had to learn new skills. I was not afraid to get back into the classroom to learn new skills," she said.

Mirie points to many myths about the limitations of retired women. Many believe that they lack relevance, tech savviness, inspiration, or motivation. But Grandma Mirie has defied all these theories. As a senior citizen, she has taken computer classes, learned to play the steel pan, learned Spanish, pottery making — demonstrating that you can reap success later in life.

"There's no expiration date on passion because retirement may just be your season to shine and pave the way for younger people. If you have health and strength, why stop doing what you enjoy?" Mirie asks.

Grandma Mirie sees herself as a voice of the past, a role model of the present and a visionary that will open doors to the future. As a lifelong learner, she is not afraid to fail. She sees failure as the mother of success and believes that failure can provide valuable lessons and opportunities for growth.

Miriam Samuel hopes to leave a legacy of hard work, courage, and confidence. Having set the bar for retired persons she hopes that they will recognize that they don't have to follow convention and feel limited by their age.

"It's all about attitude, aptitude, application and appreciation of yourself and others. Life evolves and happiness comes from recognizing who you are, what you want and what drives you. This mindset helps to channel your energy and narrow the direction you want your life to take, leading to a greater likelihood of success." Mirie said.

If you choose to start a business, Mirie advises that you demonstrate a purpose. "Today's customers want to hear your stories because they are not just buying your product, they are making an investment in you. Purpose-driven businesses are extremely attractive to female customers, because they tend to gravitate to products and services that not only solve a problem, but also serve a greater good.

As the owner of *Screw Pine,* a small enterprise she offers more than 90 different agri-products. An active gardener, she integrates the fruits of her harvest into her diverse product line. Mirie is arguably one of Antigua and Barbuda's most active entrepreneurs with the "wit, will and skill" to make a difference. But behind her success lies a challenging journey fraught with obstacles and uncertainties. She will delve deep into the ingredients necessary for entrepreneurial success, exploring the mindset, skills, strategies, and principles that pave the way toward accomplishing one's ambitions.

Despite all of her accomplishments, her role as grandma is one of Mirie's greatest achievements. It is the bridge that connects her past to the future of her 10 grandchildren and 2 great grandchildren. She believes that grandmothers should create a strong legacy for their families and communities to follow. Many lose their grandmothers before they are old enough to enjoy the love that a grandma brings. "Every house needs a grandma and my products are designed to recreate the aromas, flavours, warmth, and nostalgia of a grandma connection. Life is for living not for retiring. I want to be remembered as everyone's grandma," she said.

Mirie shares her "magic recipe for life." As a culinary creative, her practical recipes draw parallels from her mastery in the kitchen. But she cautions that everyone's recipe is unique because everyone's life circumstances are different. Her recipes reflect her personal experiences and the decisions that she made with the knowledge and information that she had at that time.

The chapters of this book are not chronological but are based on nine key characteristics identified by Miriam as the main ingredients for a rewarding life. The stories will take you on a motivational journey and offer valuable solutions for overcoming many of life's challenges.

Each chapter ends with a "Miri-ism" — an inspiring quote that summarises a particular aspect of her life. There are also journal prompts — questions designed to help readers reflect on and record their own life experiences. We hope that you will tap into Mirie's insights. We encourage you to jot down your thoughts as a part of the process of self-reflection and inspiration. As you focus on your own goals and aspirations, may this book inspire your thinking and offer a guiding light.

Please join us in wishing Grandma Mirie a Happy, Healthy 90th Birthday! May you also be inspired to love, lead and leave a legacy.

Contents

1 Entrepreneurship: Unleash your dreams and start building your empire 12

    Grandma Mirie's Simple Recipe For Success 31
    Journal Prompts 38

2 Inspire a community by believing in yourself 39

    Grandma Mirie's Sweet Bread 52
    Grandma Mirie's Banana Bread 54
    Grandma Mirie's Carrot Cake 55
    Journal Prompts 58

3 Once a teacher, forever a motivator and 'way-maker'... 59

    Grandma Mirie's Antiguan Ducana 75
    Journal Prompts 78

4 Grow your garden to multiply knowledge and resilience. 79

    Grandma Mirie's Pepperpot 89
    Journal Prompts 92

5 Transform lives through faith, hope, and hospitality 93

    Grandma Mirie's Fudge 106
    Grandma Mirie's Jellies 107
    Journal Prompts 110

6 Generosity: Love to give and give with love 111

    Grandma Mirie's Seasoned Rice......................................121
    Journal Prompts 124

7 Replenish your mind and keep reinventing your soul.125

    Grandma Mirie's Soap...133
    Grandma Mirie's Neem Oil 134
    Grandma Mirie's Wine 136
    Journal Prompts 139

8 Embrace life with boundless energy and enthusiasm. Adventure awaits! 140

    Grandma Mirie's Cassava Bread 151
    Journal Prompts 154

9 Build a legacy on a foundation of love, lessons, and leadership 155

    Grandma Mirie's Kombucha 171
    Journal Prompts 175

Final Word 176

    Serving Instructions for Rhymes in Her-Story.................. 176
    Rhyming Recipe 183

Acknowledgments 185

About the Author 186

Dedication

To my parents, John and Gertrude, my husband, Charlesworth, and my older brother Claude, who have gone before me. To my six younger siblings, Lawrence, Inger, Connie, Elliott, Muriel, and Jane. Combined, we share more than 580 years of Fleming sibling stamina!

CHAPTER 1

Entrepreneurship – Unleash your dreams and start building your empire

Some of our earliest travel experiences can inspire, motivate, and push us to big dreams. Rumour had it that we were headed to the second World War and life in the Caribbean and the entire British empire faced an aura of uncertainty and instability. Amid this crisis, the Fleming family was making plans to leave Anguilla and head to Antigua in search of a better life, on a bigger island. An established sugar and cotton producing colony with many estates, would provide better economic opportunities for our family. In relocating from Anguilla, his paternal home, to Antigua, his maternal home, Pa Fleming, had dreams of a brighter future for his children.

But this was not the first time that Pa was crossing the ocean in search of work. Just after the end of World War I, he and his sisters travelled to the Dominican Republic "to cut cane." Although he never shared details of his experience, he returned to Anguilla and his sisters remained, making the Dominican Republic their home. Many relatives and friends had also left for Panama in search of work and others had gone to America, including one of his sisters who went to Africa!

Pa's younger brother, Uncle Phillip, was doing well in Antigua and encouraged my father to move back to Antigua to find work. Born in Antigua, Pa was sent to live with relatives in Anguilla after the untimely death of his father. But life was tough. So accompanied by his wife, Gertrude, whom he married in 1931, and his young family of three children, we set sail for Antigua in January of 1938. Claude, Lawrence, and I were extremely excited about taking our first ocean voyage. Ma was pregnant with my younger sister, Inger, and so there was anticipation all around.

I looked forward to meeting my paternal grandmother in Antigua and I was excited about the 116-mile journey from Anguilla to Antigua that would take about 5 days. At 4 years old, I have only vague memories of being in the "belly of the boat" and the exhilaration that I felt as we landed in Antigua. I remember the words, "land ahead." I also remember seeing and feeling sunlight and getting out of the "hold" of the boat where we had been confined for a few days. As we boarded a bus, somewhere near High Street, in St. John's, my heart was racing. I was intrigued by the prospect of a new island, a new school, new friends, and new family. I had mixed feelings, but I also had big dreams about this new frontier that was expected to broaden my family's horizons.

I had heard many positive stories about Antigua from Pa, but I was still a bit ambivalent, not knowing what to expect. So, before we set sail, as Ma was packing "valuables" like her wedding ring, good petticoats, and important papers, I snuck some seeds into the trunk. I did not know what to expect in Antigua, so I brought seeds with me to plant in my new backyard.

January was the end of the pomme surette season and this was one of my favourite fruits. So, I had started to put away the seeds in brown paper to take with me on my journey. Just in case they did not have these fruits in Antigua, I decided that I would plant my own tree when we got to my new home. My parents were quite amused when I asked them to pack my seeds with the rest of our belongings and Pa remarked that these were called "dumb seeds." Whatever they were called, I was already dreaming of a backyard with my favourite fruit trees and a small plot of land where I could have my own "ground."

"Dumbs" trees are big, provide a lot of shade and give character to a backyard. The sight of ripe dumbs on the ground under the tree was one of my best memories of our yard. I wanted to recreate that scene in Antigua and maintain a connection to our life in Anguilla. Maybe I could even sell "dumbs," just like the women at the market. My family was going to Antigua to make more money and I was determined to do my share to contribute.

Once our family arrived in Antigua, my curiosity kicked into high gear and a dreamer was born. Antigua was bigger and more developed than Anguilla and I began to look forward to the "brighter" future that my parents had promised. I was nervous, but ready to accept the many unknowns. Dreaming fuelled a sense of creativity within me. Like any artist, musician, author, or other creative person, I was ready to learn new things and adapt to our new environment.

We settled in the village of Swetes, a stone's throw from the village of Sawcolts, where my paternal grandmother lived. My parents were hired at a nearby estate. My father became a cane cutter and my mother worked as a "grass puller" weeding the cane fields. She also worked in the cotton fields during the harvest, and because of her attention to detail, she was very good at it and highly sought after as a cotton picker. I recall going to the cotton field with her and lending a hand. I was motivated by her strong work ethic.

With two working parents, my siblings and I spent a lot of time unsupervised. I am told that a villager once stopped by to see the family and asked for my mother, my response was "Ma gone Antigua to pick cotton." Not realising that we were already in Antigua, in my small mind, I associated Antigua as a place where my parents worked.

My parents would head to the field where they worked before daybreak, and I would ensure that my younger siblings had something to eat. Life was not without struggle for our newly relocated family. With both parents working from dawn to dusk, 'big sister Mirie' had to lend a hand as a pseudo parent. By the time I was 5 years old, I would help with the family chores. I learned to cook, wash and clean and discipline my younger siblings. Instead of waiting for my mother to get home, I learned how to "catch a fire" and experimented with cooking — preparing different dishes using the crops in our backyard garden.

Once World War II began in 1939, like many other families we struggled with food shortage. But the Flemings were foragers and we survived by relying on the land. My mother did not let any of our backyard space go to waste and I remember a lot of peas and corn being planted in our backyard. My mother brought some of her own recipes from Anguilla and I remember eating corn soup quite often. When there was no corn, she made peas fungee, an Anguillan delicacy. For crops that we did not grow, we found ways to barter peas and other produce with our neighbours.

We also had cows and goats and so there was an abundance of milk which was essential for growing children. We had enough milk to sell to clients in our village and in neighbouring communities. This was also a means of generating revenue.

This experience taught me to be extremely resourceful and to find different ways to prepare the food. So whatever little we had, we could "stretch" it and make it enjoyable. I also learned the importance of community and cultivating not just crops, but good relationships with neighbours.

Of course, my pomme surette seeds had not grown and I had given up on the idea of having that big fruit tree in our backyard. However, we did plant a variety of other fruit trees, such as guavas, mangoes, and plums to ensure that we always had something to eat.

As we continued through the war, I often heard my parents say that they were happy that we left Anguilla when we did, because regional travel had become more difficult, and we were facing even tougher economic times. But my mother seemed very concerned about our family's future and she missed her family and friends that she had left behind in Anguilla. I recall when she got a letter telling her that her mother, Emily had passed away. My mother was a tough woman, and it was extremely difficult to see her cry.

But I never lost sight of that vision of a brighter future in Antigua that my family sought after. But I often wondered how life would have been different for my family, had we stayed in Anguilla. Twelve years passed before my mother returned to Anguilla for a visit in 1950. Despite her concerns about the war and our family's economic future, she accepted Antigua as her new home – a place where she could fulfil her dreams of a better life. I remember having great admiration for my mother's resourcefulness and how she planned for a rainy day by always putting food and money aside.

By my teenage years, I was largely running the household. World War II had ended by the time I turned 11, but financially, things were still tough on our family. Sugar was Antigua's main industry and my parents continued to toil in a struggling economy, facing food rations and uncertain employment. They were in a very vulnerable position and moved around to different estates in search of work. These included: Willis Freeman, Morris Looby and DeLapps. If the island faced a drought or storm activity, it meant that my parents could be furloughed. I quickly recognized the importance of food security, having gone to bed many nights on an empty stomach.

I played a key role in the upkeep of the family's backyard garden, learning more about the planting and reaping season for a variety of crops, to ensure that my siblings and I would always have something to eat. This was where my cooking adventures began as I experimented with food preparation and sharpened my problem-solving skills and creativity. "Thinking outside of the box" became a survival tool in my quest to ensure that my 7 siblings and I could survive. I discovered my love for baking, during Home Economics Class. My teacher was the legendary tastemaker, Dame Gwendolyn Tongue, who helped to unlock and nurture my passion for the culinary arts. I was taught by the best!

My mother always talked about "bettering yourself" and that she had come to Antigua for a better life. I was a good student and very competitive. After completing my schooling at All Saints School, I entered the teaching profession in 1954/55. My father also died that year after a brief illness and that placed even greater financial pressure on my mother. My father had dreams of me becoming a teacher and having a profession, but unfortunately, he died before the start of my teaching career.

My first teaching assignment was at the All Saints School where I taught for almost one term. I was transferred to the Liberta School, where I taught for nine years. My meagre starting salary of $24 per month did not come close to providing the financial freedom that I had envisioned, especially since I now had to contribute to the family finances. So, I continued to work in the backyard garden to supplement feeding myself and my family. Although I had landed my dream job, I quickly recognized the need to develop additional streams of income. This was my first lesson in financial literacy, and I had to come up with a budget to cover my monthly expenses.

In 1962 I married Charlesworth Samuel, a fellow villager. I was attracted to his humility and his drive. Our son Clement was born in November 1963, a week before the assassination of President Kennedy. Thirteen months after that, our daughter Derede arrived and thirteen months after that Megan our second daughter was born.

We were assigned to the newly opened John Hughes Primary School. My husband was the Principal and I was a senior teacher. We lived in the school house and started an on-site garden that was supported by the entire community. This strengthened our ties with the villagers. Many came to partake of the fruits and vegetables, which we lovingly shared. There was no bread shop in the village at that time. With a family of three young children, it became more economical and convenient to bake bread for my family. This became a favourite pastime and as my passion for baking grew. I happily shared bread with many villagers as well.

In the Caribbean, nothing says home, like the smell of baking and the act of "breaking bread" with friends and family. Although my baked goods were free for all to enjoy, the positive feedback and compliments that I received from "potential" clients fuelled my creativity and helped to build my confidence. My husband also believed in what I was doing and would often remark that when you do what you love, the rewards will come.

Our home in John Hughes became a gathering spot for many students who knew there was always something to eat. Our ties with this community continued to blossom and we would discover 45 years later just how great our reward would be. This very school was renamed *Hon. Charlesworth T Samuel Primary* to honour my late husband, the school's first headmaster and later Parliamentary representative. I accept this designation on his behalf as a part of our shared legacy.

My husband's dream of pursuing higher education would become the breeding ground for my dreams as well. In 1966, his dream of pursuing higher education became a reality and he headed to the University of the West Indies (UWI) Barbados in September of that year.

Political instability in Antigua was a growing concern for our family. A radicalised working class was emerging which eventually led to George Walter breaking ranks with the Antigua and Barbuda Trade and Labour Union (AT&LU). It seemed like there was a strike or picket every month. My husband, a political junkie, tracked the developments closely. He predicted that things would come to a head and was extremely nervous about leaving his young family behind. Outraged by the "declaration of war against Antiguan workers" Charlesworth Samuel relocated his family because of the unstable political climate.

In January 1967, my family boarded the Federal Maple, one of the cargo/passenger island-hopping ships that served the Caribbean region. As we settled in the "hold" of the boat which had the capacity to carry 200 passengers, a feeling of déjà vu came over me. It had been almost 30 years since my family had embarked on a similar journey from Anguilla to Antigua. The mixed feelings of ambivalence and anticipation that I felt as I travelled to a new country years before, came rushing back. Except this time, I was the parent spearheading the dream.

As I looked at my three children, I remembered how my first journey had awakened dreams that were later unleashed. I could only imagine the thoughts that were racing through the minds of my three children. I thought about my parents and wondered what was going through their minds as they took that courageous trip with their three children, in search of better economic opportunities.

Although our circumstances were different, once I recognized that I was following a similar path to my parents, a feeling of confidence came over me. I had done this before. The same God who had watched over my family three decades prior, would also protect my family. I understood my assignment and I was ready to "throw caution to the wind" and give it my all.

Three months after we left Antigua, workers from every sector of the economy except essential services, went on strike. The economy came to a halt and the Defence Force was called out. What started out as workers' demand for the right to belong to a trade union, escalated to a national strike, a state of emergency and the eventual demand for the government's resignation in 1968. It turned out that my husband's worst fears had come true.

As we settled in Barbados, 5 weeks after the country gained political independence, my husband was extremely impressed with the new style of governance and declared that this was his vision for Antigua. He vowed that he would not return to Antigua until there was a change in government. After more than 15 years of the same government, I was not sure what he meant at the time. But that was a dream and affirmation that he repeated often and so it also became my dream.

Against a backdrop of empowered citizens in Barbados, a newly independent nation, I got the courage to consider turning my "passion into profits." In this newly independent country, there were so many opportunities for personal development and growth and this gave me a new perspective on life.

Facing financial challenges, I adapted quickly to our new surroundings and decided to "try my hand" in entrepreneurship. I took advantage of many free craft classes that were available to the public. Very soon, I began to market crochet hats and bags to supplement our family income. I also began baking my own version of Bajan sweet bread, returning to my love for baking, while immersing myself in the local culture. The ability to pivot swiftly in response to unexpected hurdles can spell the difference between success and failure.

There is something empowering about adapting to a new environment. It helped to unleash my ideas and my dreams began to hatch. Dreams can broaden our horizons and provide the roadmap for our ideas as a constant reminder that we can achieve whatever we put our minds to. Without dreams, the journey of any entrepreneur lacks meaning, inspiration and direction.

The best dreamers are always curious and hyper-aware. We solve problems and come up with unique solutions that others may not see or recognize. I let my imaginations soar, but I always keep one foot planted on the ground, because dreams require a lot of work and effort.

An entrepreneurial journey almost always begins with a dream but some allow the fear of failure to overcome the execution of their dream. Others jump in without preparation. The key to successfully starting a business lies in the process of nurturing your dream. Allow it to develop. Invest time and effort. Start by taking baby steps.

As a lifelong dreamer, here are some of the things I've learned that might be helpful to those looking to pursue entrepreneurship:

"Don't put all your dreams in one basket."

Do not expect that the stars will always align and that *all* your dreams will come true. Don't pin all your hopes on any one dream. Constantly cultivate new ideas and interests in the pipeline.

"Forward Thinking".

Always try to be several steps ahead, several moves in advance, and think several years into the future. Like a chess game, you must think several moves ahead, to successfully cultivate the habit of dreaming big. Today's entrepreneurs must harness the power of digital tools to not just keep up with the times but to propel their business into the future.

"Unshakable Belief in God and Helping Others"

You must have faith that whatever you can conceptualise in your mind, you can realise in the physical world. For me, a spiritual connection to God and a deep belief in humanity motivates me to multiply my talents by helping others. The best dreams are not only for my advancement but they are also designed to help raise others.

"Use Empowering Language"

The language you use daily should affirm your dreams and reflect your thoughts. My words cannot be riddled with complaining, worrying, and criticising life circumstances. I use empowering words and phrases that are focused on solutions, ideas, and expanding possibilities.

We empower our lives by our narrative. I always speak positivity into existence.

Integrity, Trust, and Customer Service

Integrity is the cornerstone of business and will earn the trust and loyalty of customers. By prioritising customer satisfaction and feedback, as an entrepreneur you can continually refine your products to meet their needs and preferences. This will help generate positive word-of-mouth, which is priceless for a growing business.

"Big Ideas, Plans, and Goals"

When laying out a plan of action, never settle for the status quo. Instead set goals that will expand your comfort zone, push limits, and stretch your imagination. The best dreamers know that life is too short for small dreams.

We plant a seed when we begin to dream. For many entrepreneurs, starting a business is the culmination of many years of dreaming and planning. Being adventurous also makes the dream sweeter. If we are willing to take risks, make sacrifices, try new things then our dreams become adventures.

At an early age, cooking took me on an adventure to experiment with new flavours using backyard ingredients, as a means of survival. This set a pattern throughout the rest of my career as a teacher, to continue my creative pursuits through cooking and craft. I was able to supplement my income with several side hustles.

In my ninth decade, I still approach life as a dreamer but I am driven more by passion than profits. I often ask myself, what unmet need am I passionate about? What unique idea can I come up with to meet that need? Then I follow my dream, knowing that when you do what you love, the rewards will come.

DREAMING IS A HABIT TO BE CULTIVATED AND THEN EXECUTED!

Grandma Mirie's Simple Recipe for Success

1 Cup of good thoughts

1 Cup of kind deeds

2 Cups of well beaten faults

1 Cup of consideration for others

3 Cups of ideas

1 spoonful of elbow grease

A pinch of self-confidence

Directions:

Mix all ingredients thoroughly and moisten by adding tears of joy, sorrow, and sympathy for others. For lumps and bumps, add extra determination to taste.

Fold in 4 cups of prayer and faith to lighten other ingredients and raise the texture to greater heights.

Pour all this batter into your family and friends and let the mixture sit uncovered to settle. Bake well with the heat of human kindness.

Serve with a smile. Store memories in your heart.

The recipe will be a little bit different for everyone because we don't all have the same palette and we all have different cravings. But this is where you start to put your spin on the recipe for entrepreneurship.

Let's dig in!

MIRIE'S MEMORABLE MOMENTS

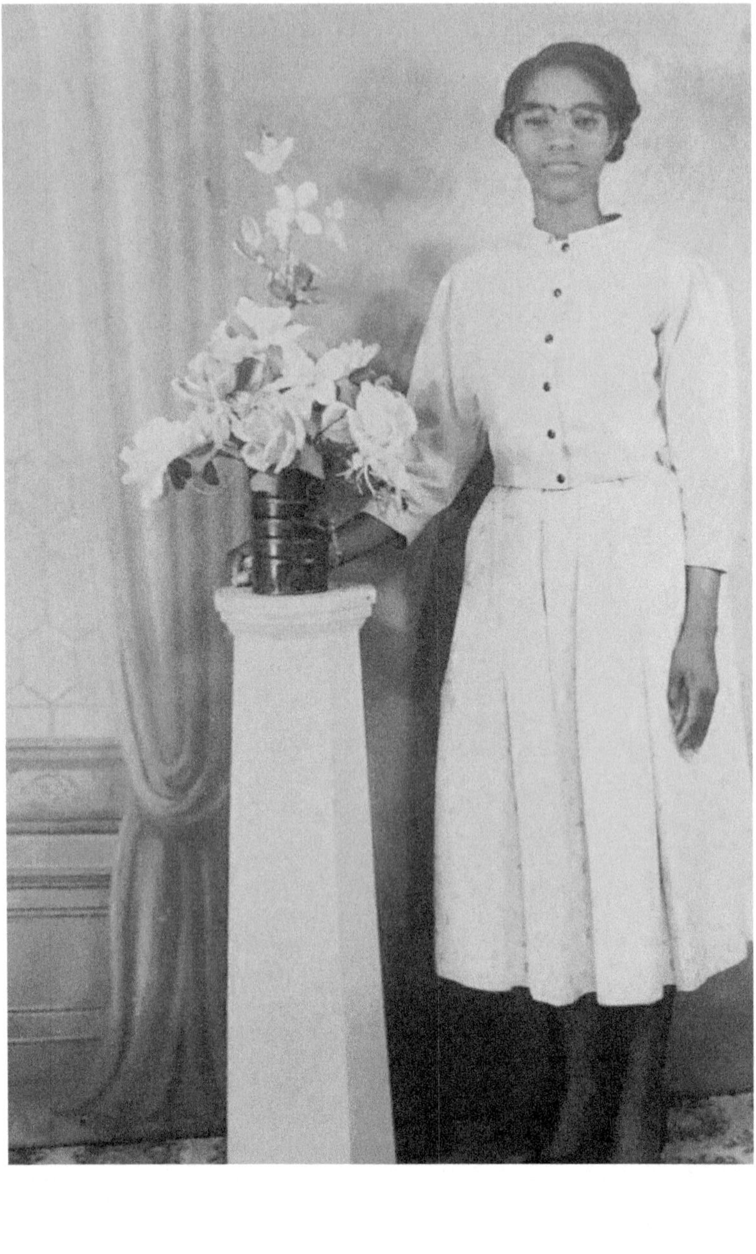

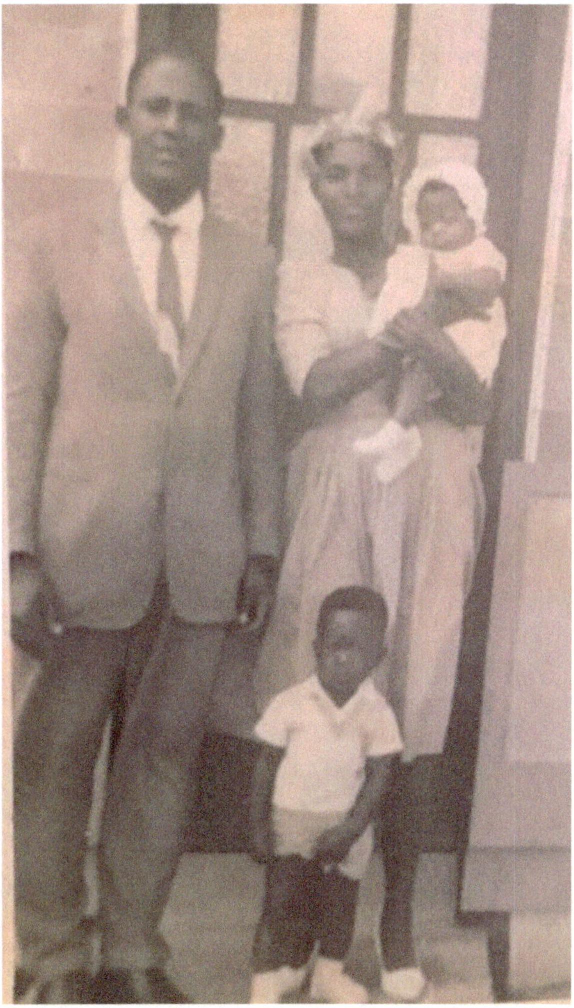

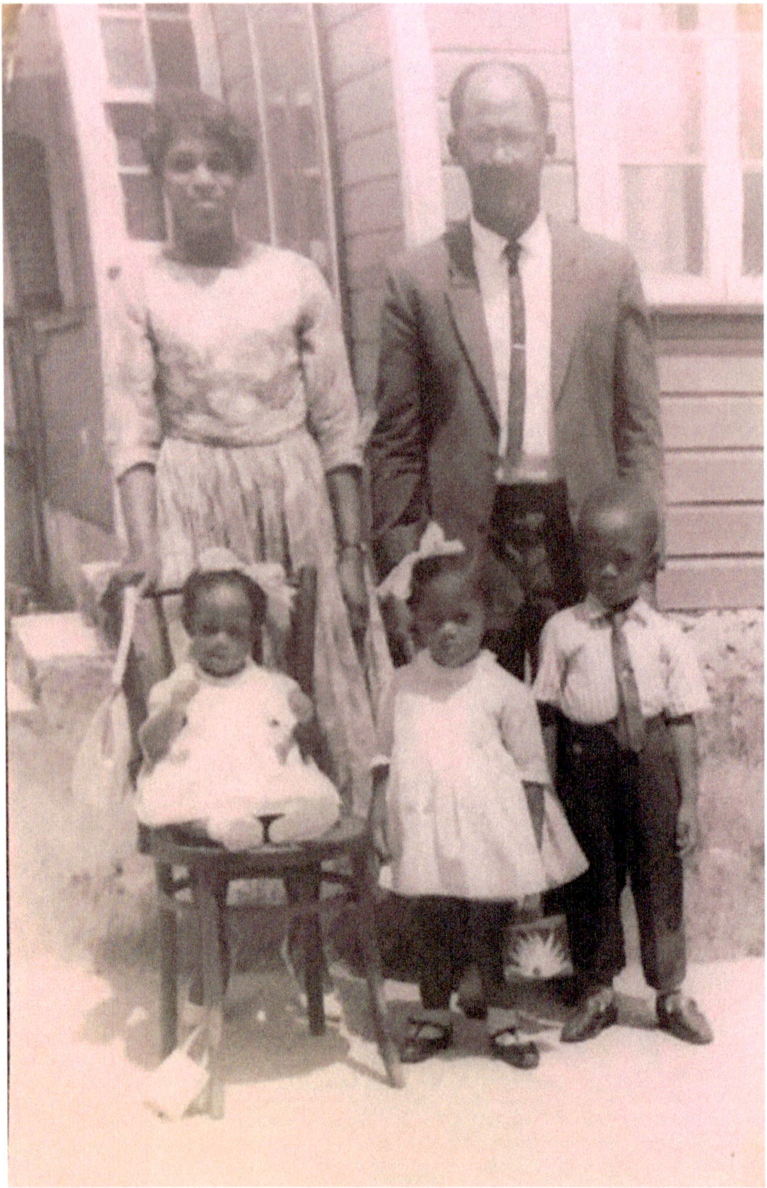

MIRI-ISM

> Even if you're on the right track,
> you'll get run over
> if you just sit there.
>
> MIRIAM SAMUEL TURNS 90

Journal Prompts

1. What does "dreaming big" mean to you? How do you define your goals and aspirations?

2. List three tangible steps that would bring you closer to one of your biggest dreams. How can you start taking actions towards your goals?

CHAPTER 2

Inspire a community by believing in yourself

God has given to each of us gifts as unique as our fingerprints. Of the 8 billion people on this planet, no one else on earth is quite like you. That means you have something unique to contribute to this world. You're neither insignificant nor unimportant.

One of the most important lessons I've learnt in life is to believe in me. Self-belief is important. It's the source of confidence to try new things and take risks. It keeps you going in challenging times and in the face of disappointment. You refuse to take 'No' for an answer and it fuels creativity and a can-do attitude. We all need it. Trust me on this one.

In January 1967 our young family moved to Barbados to join my husband. He had enrolled at the University of the West Indies in September and travelled ahead of the family to secure accommodations. He returned to Antigua for Christmas and just after the New

Year, my husband, our 3 children and I, travelled on the Federal Maple ship to Bridgetown. Sailing with three young children, who were 3 years old and under, and all our possessions that we could carry, including my husband's car, was the start of an important chapter in the life of our family.

This was an era of transformation throughout the free world. Let me set the scene. Only weeks before we arrived, Barbados had gained its political independence from the British Empire in November 1966. It was the third Caribbean island to do so, alongside a wave of former colonies across the globe throughout the 1960s. In the decade between 1956 and 1966 more than two dozen new countries were created from the dying embers of the British Empire. A global sense of freedom and empowerment was in the air!

Our reason for moving to Barbados was that the University College of the West Indies gained full university status in 1962 and a campus opened in Barbados in 1963. My husband, already a Head Teacher, had been successful in securing a UWI scholarship from the Mill Reef Club in Antigua. So, his dream of pursuing higher education became the family's dream. At the time, most people in the Caribbean did not have a secondary school education, so an opportunity for university education put us among a very privileged few and positioned our family among the intelligentsia of the region.

Similar to what my parents had done almost 30 years earlier, we left behind our home, our families, and careers for another country and culture which was more advanced than our own. Antigua did not gain limited self-governance until November 1967 and would not gain its independence until 1981. So, we left behind a colony, and landed in a brand-new country full of optimism and hope. We settled among citizens who were beaming with national pride. Nearly 6 years would pass before we returned to Antigua and during our residency in Barbados not only were we witnesses to the birth of a new nation, but I also gave birth to my fourth child.

The three older children enrolled in their first school, Pine Primary, and the entire family became a part of the "Pride of Barbados." The world changed rapidly during our Bajan residency and I became more attentive to the news from Antigua and around the world. Once you leave your homeland, your ears are always on alert, awaiting updates on what was happening back home. There was talk about a possible uprising in Antigua and my husband was tuned into the political developments.

As far as international news, my horizons were quickly broadening as I adjusted my mindset to better process world events and news. We witnessed the Arab-Israeli Six Day War in 1967 which set the stage for middle east conflict for the next two generations. Martin Luther King was assassinated in 1968, Neil Armstrong set foot on the moon in 1969, the Beatles disbanded in 1970 the same week as the failed attempt of Apollo 13. Walt Disney World opened in 1971, and the final manned mission to the moon was launched in 1972 during which the famous 'blue marble' image of the earth was taken.

Of lesser world importance, but of greater personal significance to me, I learned to drive and have continued to do so in the 56 years since I passed my driving test. Now that was the ultimate state of independence since most of the women in my circle at the time, did not drive! Women in Antigua were granted the right to vote in 1951, and I was also among the first women in my circle to boldly exercise my franchise. I also voted in the 1971 general elections in Barbados, having been a resident on the island for more than 3 years. In many ways, the move to Barbados was an exercise in self-improvement and personal development as my confidence continued to grow.

We had to adapt to a new culture, social structure, and different lifestyle. With no family or close friends to lean on, we trusted God to find all the resources and support that we needed to make a fresh start in this new setting. One of the most treasured wedding gifts that we received was a painting with the scripture "But my God shall supply all your needs according to his riches in glory by Christ Jesus." Philippians 4.19. This painting, proudly displayed in our living room, became a daily source of strength and affirmation for our family.

We had moved from the small rural village of John Hughes in Antigua where my husband was the inaugural Head Teacher of a newly opened primary school and I was one of the senior teachers, to a heady new community in the Pine Area. We became a part of a mixed urban community that comprised the working class to university elites, all looking to make their contributions to one of the newly emerging nations of the Caribbean.

The Bajans loved their flag and national anthem ... "In plenty and in times of need, when this fair land was young, our great forefathers sowed the seeds, from which our pride was sprung." Remember, when we left Antigua, the island was still a colony and our national anthem and flag had not yet been introduced. We were still singing, "God Save the Queen." My husband who had been politically active since the age of 15, revelled in the wave of patriotism that was sweeping through Barbados. It was an empowering experience and I felt a part of a community of go-getters. I felt that I could accomplish anything that I set my mind to do.

But I had travelled a similar road before with my parents, and despite the uncertainty before us, I had faith and confidence that we would make it. I harkened back to the tenacity and resourcefulness of my mother, as I watched her toil to provide for our family. I recalled how she chose her friends and allies carefully. I was determined to be just as deliberate in my actions to make the necessary changes to confront the challenges ahead.

While there was much to learn, there were meagre resources to draw upon. My husband, the former school principal, was now a UWI student and taught part-time to make ends meet. I also worked as a teacher at the Modern High School and created lasting friendships with some of my colleagues who welcomed me and my family into their social circles. As my list of friends expanded so did my self-confidence. We attended the White Park Pilgrim Holiness Church in Bridgetown and joined a vibrant faith community. As we became more active in the church, we met new friends and this fast tracked our integration into our new community.

We connected with other families through the university networks and exchanged stories about our struggles and sacrifices. I also joined the Parent Teacher Association (PTA) at Pine Primary School and became active in the Girl Guide and Boy Scout Associations. Through these networks, I developed great relationships with teachers as well as parents and this strengthened my ties to this community.

With a limited budget for clothing, I began to make crochet hats and bags, first for myself and then for close friends. I learned to crochet as a child by watching my mother. After attending crochet classes at a community centre in Bridgetown, I learned to use patterns, and approached the art form as a professional. I started selling my creations to my church family and word quickly spread. My fashion line became a hit at many weddings, social events, and national exhibitions in a country where the concept of "locally made" products was a growing phenomenon. In the process, I discovered a new level of independence and generated a new source of income and a growing client base, who validated my hard work with their repeat business and referrals.

One of the things I also learned was how to make what Barbadians (Bajans) call sweet bread. The rest of the world might know it as coconut bread. However, sweet bread is in fact neither a bread nor a cake. It's somewhere in between. Hugely popular in Barbados, it was less common in Antigua back in the 60s. The closest thing to sweet bread that I knew of was the Antiguan "rock cake." But despite the similarities in taste, the textures were very different.

Sweet bread is delicious. Other parts of the world pioneered carrot cake and banana bread, but coconut bread comes from the Caribbean and the Americas. It's one of our gifts to the world. So, I was keen to learn how to master making sweet bread like a Bajan, which I did. At the end of this chapter see my recipe for what I believe is the best sweet bread you'll find.

However, having learned to make sweet bread from the best, I was nonetheless convinced that the recipe could be improved. So, I aimed to do just that. Looking back now, I can see that this was itself a small indication of self-belief. Despite being a "foreigner in a brave new world", learning to make a local delicacy from those who made it best, I was bold enough to believe that I could add something to the mix to enhance this product.

The result is that my sweet bread isn't quite like the ones sold in bakeries and served in front rooms and church halls across Barbados. It has a crumblier texture, as the coconut is more coarsely grated. My version is less dense and the larger coconut shavings give it a rougher topping. I think it's a great recipe, refined through trial and error, and over the years I've made and sold *a lot* of sweet bread. *A lot!* It's arguably my number one product and 50 years later, my coconut bread still graces the shelves of many supermarkets across Antigua.

Making sweet bread and refining your own recipe taught me a lot about believing in myself.

Cultivating self-belief means that you don't have to follow some else's recipe or someone else's playbook in order to have a successful outcome. You can follow your own path and still have a successful outcome. Indeed, I'd go further to say that by following your own path you will have a unique sense of accomplishment and self-actualization, regardless of the outcome.

There's a difference between arrogance and self-belief. It's arrogant to believe that you have nothing to learn from others. We all have much to learn. Indeed, in the final chapter of this book I'll go on to advocate that we all should keep on learning. Nonetheless, once we've learned from others, we understand that we don't have to be limited by the ideas and knowledge that we've received. It's part of our individuality to ask, 'What do I bring to this table? How can I mix it up a little differently? How do my gifts shape what I've learnt from others so that my fingerprints are on this as much as those on whose shoulders I stand?'

So, when you make your own sweet bread from my recipe, (in fact put down the book and go do it now) don't feel you can't diverge from my recipe. This is just my way of making sweet bread. Once you understand it, do it your way. Believe in yourself. Try something new.

Making sweet bread, especially your own customized version, teaches you about self-belief in at least 4 ways:

First, you'll come to believe that there's no such thing as failure. Instead, think of it as trial and error. Eventually, if you keep trying it will all work out. Every error teaches you what not to do the next time round, so that your chances of success improve with each new attempt. The only way to fail is to give up. If you believe in yourself, you will get there eventually.

Second, believe deeply that only you get to determine what success looks like for you. Not anyone else. Never delegate to someone else the power to determine what counts as your success.

By way of example, as a working mother in Barbados with three young children, joined by a fourth child a few short years later, climbing the teaching career ladder was never my measure of success. For me, success at that time was measured in achieving personal goals like learning to drive, making sure our children were well fed, clothed, educated, and socialized.

Third, never cease to believe that you're as good as anybody else. Even if they have more experience. One of the upsides of determining for yourself what success looks like for you, is that you never need to compare yourself to anyone else.

Fourth, refuse to believe that there are limits to how far you can go. You've no idea how far self-belief might take you. Learning to make sweet bread in Barbados and developing my own twist on the recipe meant I could eventually sell it in Antigua as authentic Bajan sweet bread and make a name for myself while doing it. Sweet bread became the first product that I sold — my starter product. It remains one of my most popular products. So, my sweet bread became a fusion of 2 cultures, Bajan and Antiguan and an important emblem in achieving "mental and financial independence." The courage to open my own business is somehow rooted in the way I was able to transform a Bajan tradition for Antiguan consumption. I believed in myself and I encourage everyone to venture deep and believe in yourself too.

My son Calvin was born in 1969 and my husband graduated from the Cave Hill Campus in 1972 with a degree in Natural Sciences. With a new government in place, our expanded family began to make plans to relocate to our home in Antigua. As I sailed once again towards our new horizon, that familiar mixed feeling of anticipation and ambivalence came over me. But I was returning to Antigua with an additional child, and more confidence and maturity. My path to entrepreneurship had begun and I had a new product to introduce to the Antiguan market. I was taking a piece of Barbados with me. Although it was not a plant, the Antigua-Bajan bread market was about to grow.

Nothing could have fully prepared me for the next chapter in the life of my family. But the burst of confidence that came with the self-belief that I had cultivated, would go a long way in empowering me to face the mountains that lay ahead.

Grandma Mirie's Sweet Bread

1 lb flour

1 coconut grated

½ cup milk

1 egg

½ lb sugar

¼ lb melo cream

1 tsp essence

1 tbsp baking powder

¼ lb melo cream

2 oz raisins

Cinnamon

Nutmeg

Cherries for topping

Method:

1. Melt melo cream - combine flour, sugar, and baking powder in a bowl - add melo cream. Use fingers or pastry mincer to work in the melo cream.

2. Add coconut, raisins, and mix well.

3. Add eggs, milk, essence, cinnamon and nutmeg and fold in, if necessary add a little water.

4. Pour in a greased load pan and bake at 350dregrees F in a preheated oven for 1 hour.

Grandma Mirie's Banana Bread

2 ripe bananas

½ cup milk

1 tbsp lemon juice

2 eggs

1 tsp baking soda

½ tsp salt

¼ lb butter

½ lb flour

⅓ lb sugar

Nuts of your choice

Method:

1. Mix banana and lemon juice together. Add nuts and remaining ingredients - mix well.

2. Pour into a greased loaf pan and bake at 350degreesF in a preheated oven for about 1 hr.

Grandma Mirie's Carrot Cake

¾ lb flour

2 tsp baking powder

2 tsp cinnamon

5 eggs

2 cups grated carrots

½ cup chopped nuts

1 ½ tsp baking soda

½ lb sugar

1 cup oil

8oz crushed pineapple

Method:
1. Mix dry ingredients
2. Add oil and beat well until light and fluffy
3. Add egg one at a time
4. Add carrots, pineapple, and nuts
5. Bake at 375F for 30-35 mins

MIRI-ISM

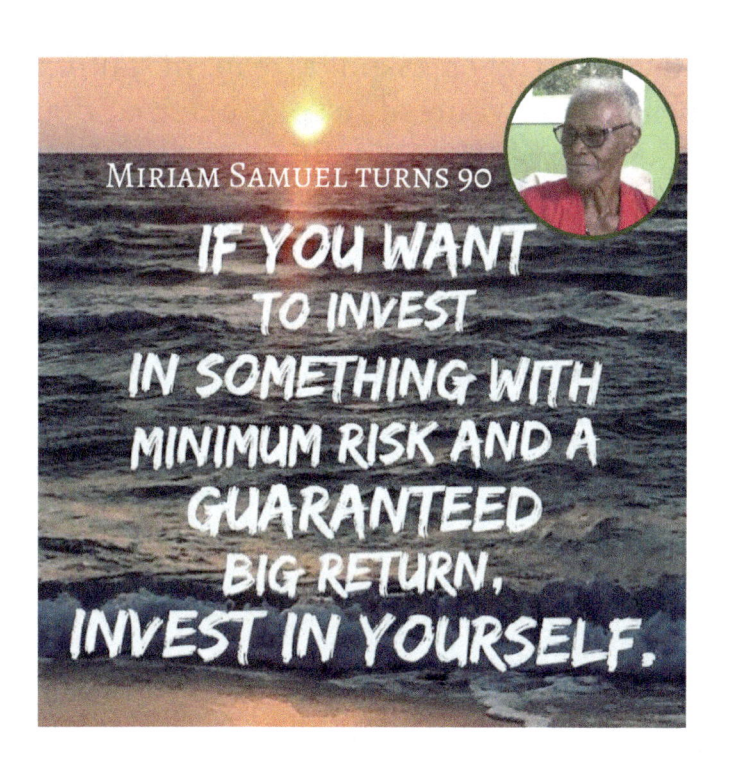

Miriam Samuel turns 90

IF YOU WANT TO INVEST IN SOMETHING WITH MINIMUM RISK AND A GUARANTEED BIG RETURN, INVEST IN YOURSELF.

Journal Prompts

1. Have you ever taken a leap of faith and believed in yourself despite external doubts or criticisms. How did this experience impact your self-confidence and resilience?

2. Visualise your ideal self as confident and resilient. What mindset shifts would help you implement this version of you?

CHAPTER 3

Once a teacher, forever a motivator and "way-maker"

When you've been around for nine decades you eventually acquire lots of names, monikers, and titles. I'm a wife, widow, mother, cousin, aunt, neighbour, and friend. I'm grandma to my grandchildren and great grandchildren, and to many of their friends. But the title by which most people know me is "Teacher Mirie."

One of the many privileges of a long life is running into people or their descendants that you've helped along the way, often in ways unknown to you at the time. For me, this happens most commonly with former students. More recent students call me Mrs Samuel, but most from the early days of my l career call me Teacher Mirie or Teacher Fleming (my maiden name). For me, the title of Teacher is not so much a description of my profession, it's my identity. Teaching is part of who I am and part of my personal history.

As a young girl growing up in a small village, teaching was a highly respected profession. A poor child from a rural community in the 1940s was not a likely candidate for a teaching career. I wanted to become a nurse. But I found every door to nursing closed. My father had declared when I was very young that I would become a teacher. He was ridiculed in some quarters for having that dream. But maybe my father's prediction and the role that I played as big sister to seven siblings, gave me permission to dream beyond my station. And against the odds, I did become a teacher on the 7$^{th\ of}$ February 1955.

When people say you can't do something, remember that's an indication of the limitations of their imagination, not yours. Speaking of limitations, one of the things I learned from my pupils is never to judge potential too quickly. I remember one primary school pupil who showed very little interest in school, partly because he'd had a negative experience with a previous teacher. I gave him the job to collect the attendance registers for my class each day. This assignment of responsibility gave him a reason to take his lessons seriously. He eventually did so well that he excelled at school and gained a scholarship to secondary school. He's now a senior police officer. No one, including me, could have seen that potential when he was a young child.

Your light as a teacher is a double-edged sword. It has the power to eclipse the Moon, but it also has the power to make the Moon shine. The Moon reflects the light of the Sun, which is pretty much what students do. They reflect our light and wisdom, which allows them to shine brighter than the North Star!

Between 1955 and my retirement in 1994, I taught in 10 different schools, 9 in Antigua and 1 in Barbados. I'm pretty confident I've taught in a greater number of schools than any other living teacher in Antigua. I also taught in 4 of our 6 parishes in Antigua, which means that I encountered students from two thirds of the island.

One of the schools where I taught for almost a decade was the Liberta School, in the largest village on the island. As an inexperienced 20-year-old, many parents saw my vulnerability and treated me as one of their children. I can recall going to homes like Aunt Vi after school, a very warm environment. I would socialise with students and their parents before taking my walk home to Swetes.

I encountered a cross section of families in Liberta. Whereas some had an economic advantage, all the parents in this community worked together to ensure that teachers were supported and respected. I often had many open invitations from parents to join their family for lunch. I looked forward to parents' offerings of mangoes, oranges, or plums as a token of their gratitude. Despite limited opportunities, achievement gaps, insufficient resources, teachers were the drivers of empowerment — sculptors of the future, moulding and shaping young minds.

I have made some lifelong friends and still have a sisterly or brotherly relationship with many students after 70 years. I recently attended the 60th Anniversary of the Liberta Primary School. I had an opportunity to speak to a packed room of attendees. I asked all my former students to stand. To my surprise, many of my former students were either past or current teachers at Liberta Primary School, including the Head Teacher! I felt proud that many of the seeds that I had planted had borne fruit and I was happy that so many of my students had followed my path and had become teachers.

Beyond the primary mission of education, teachers were at the centre of social, recreational, and cultural life in the community. Wearing many different hats, a teacher was an esteemed pillar of the community, a role model for children and parents alike.

But I was not afraid to stand up and defend my profession as a teacher. Fighting for myself meant defending my students and colleagues. I was proud to be a part of history as a participant in the Teacher's strike of 1979. Many benefits that teachers enjoy today started with industrial action. One contentious issue at the time was a policy that barred unwed female teachers who became pregnant from the classroom. They would have to leave the job, reapply after the birth of the baby, and could potentially lose their years of service. At a time when they needed the most support, unwed mothers were marginalised. No similar policy applied to unwed fathers.

I first became active in the Antigua Union of Teachers (AUT) when my husband, Charlesworth Samuel served as President for 2 years. He was succeeded by Juno Samuel. While involved in discussions with the government, Samuel was transferred from teaching to the Ministry of Economics in 1977. This was a move designed to prevent him from taking part in a contentious discussion about a new employment package. Members of the Antigua Union of Teachers (AUT) continued to protest his transfer into 1978 and on 7th of June, a group of teachers picketed the Ministry of Economics. Thirteen teachers were arrested and charged under an old colonial law *"watching and besetting."* They were tried on 13th of June 1978 and the Court dismissed the charges.

But these teachers were prevented from re-entering their classrooms by the police and remained unemployed. On January 1st of 1979, these teachers, all less than 40 years of age, were retired in the "public interest". Students attempted to stage a demonstration in support of their teachers at the Parliament building at the old Queen Elizabeth Hall. They were chased away by the Defence Force and on the 13th of January 1979, the strike began. On February 27th ACLM, AWU and the AUT planned a demonstration. But as we lined up ready to march, the Riot Squad appeared and without warning teargassed demonstrators. The strike continued until April 17th, 1979.

I returned to the classroom at Clare Hall Secondary School to face a retaliatory transfer because of my involvement in the teacher's strike. This is the only school in my teaching career that was within walking distance from my home, which I loved. I was sent to Swetes Primary on the opposite side of the island. As you might imagine, it was not a welcome move and one of the lowest points of my career.

I loved being a teacher in the community where I lived, and it was hugely convenient as a working mother to have a short walking commute from home to work. In addition, the move from a secondary to primary school felt like a retrograde step, as my teaching career had begun in primary level, and I had moved to the secondary level.

So, I was very sad to leave Clare Hall Secondary. But more than sad, I was angry. Mostly, it was the way it was done that infuriated me. I was unceremoniously transferred in the middle of a term without the courtesy of even being informed. Although my new school had been informed of my transfer, no one bothered to tell me! My abrupt transfer, without consultation or communication, seemed deliberately designed to be disruptive. I did not have the opportunity to say goodbye to my colleagues or students. Although I had not been fired, it certainly felt that way. But if the strategy was intended to frustrate me, in the hope that I might resign or abandon teaching in the public sector for the private sector, it failed. I stood firm.

At this point I was approaching my 25th anniversary as a teacher and I was prepared to defend my reputation in a profession that I had worked hard for. It would be hugely inconvenient to get to Swetes School when I had 5 children of my own, including a 5-year-old. In fact, we only had one car at the time so I ended up taking public transportation to and from work. But Swetes is the village in which I grew up, so I adjusted my mindset. I looked forward to doing my job, reconnecting with many people in that community that I loved and making a difference in the lives of many children and families.

Teaching for me is not only about passing on knowledge. That is, of course, essential. It's also about caring for the wellbeing of the children and connecting with the families and the communities from which they come. So, you become a "way-maker" to students providing whatever they need most — a friend, confidante, surrogate parent, grandparent, or counsellor as needed. And where a pupil has a need, as a teacher, it is a sacred duty to do my best to meet that need. Often there was no one else to do it.

Growing up I had some great teachers like the late Teacher Madge, Teacher Irene Williams, and Head Teacher Christopher O'Marde who went beyond their call of duty to "hold my hand." I was determined to provide that type of mentorship to my students.

So, when I meet former students, many thank me, but not for what I taught them in the classroom. That's not what they tend to remember. They thank me for providing them with food or friendship or school uniforms, or a listening ear when they were in a difficult place.

At my final school, Ottos Comprehensive, where I taught for 14 years, former students mostly remember me for food. I was asked to reactivate the school canteen and I began selling baked chicken and other savoury treats during the lunch break. School teachers are poorly paid and more so thirty years ago when I retired. In addition, I discovered that one of the blessings of selling food is that when students came to school hungry I was able to provide them with home cooked food and they could pay me whatever they could afford that day. Some couldn't afford to pay anything and were willing to work in the cafeteria in exchange for food. There were many children that I was able to help from families that were struggling financially. I remember what it was like being poor and going to school hungry. So it gave me joy that I could be a blessing to these students. It was a privilege to be able to pay forward some of my debt of gratitude.

One of the most important things that I did as a craft teacher was to expose students to practices that are deeply rooted in our history, culture, and traditions. Many of these are skills that would have otherwise been in danger of being forgotten. In my retirement, I continue to pass on this knowledge to anyone willing to learn.

This type of "hands-on" teaching and learning helps to forge strong links to our past and affirms our identity. I teach techniques like traditional palm weaving, which in former generations would have been passed down from mother to daughter. But I also teach informally, for example, by sharing what I know about the medicinal benefits of certain plants and herbs, which again would in previous generations have been carefully curated and preserved from generation to generation.

One informal way in which my identity as a teacher of our history and culture is expressed, is in the sharing of recipes, especially traditional Caribbean foods.

Antigua has a number of national dishes, deeply rooted in our history as formerly enslaved people, primarily of West African ancestry. Transported from the continent, we brought with us vestiges of our culture and food which were transplanted into Caribbean soil and fused with the Amerindian traditions of the people who preceded the enslaved Africans in the Caribbean. Visitors from West Africa will find familiar our Antiguan dishes of Fungee and saltfish, Pepper Pot, Sweet dumplin' and, of course, Ducana. A very similar dish can be found across many Caribbean islands as well as in Ghana today, where it's called dokono.

Those who know and love ducana will have very strong views about whether authentic ducana should include or exclude raisins. Let's get this out the way early on. My personal view is this: you go ahead and make your ducana in any way that pleases you and your family and tell everybody else to mind their own business! However, I do encourage you to use banana leaves to wrap your ducana. Now that's where the real authenticity begins. To me, the banana leaves represent the close-knit community that binds all of the key ingredients together.

Ducana and saltfish, ideally served with 'chop up' and plantains is a hugely popular dish. However, there's a downside. Ducana can be a pretty labour-intensive dish to prepare. So, it's not surprising that many of our younger generation rarely make this dish themselves. Those who live in Antigua can easily buy this meal from any number of vendors who make it extremely well. However, if you're not fortunate enough to live on the island or if you simply want to learn to make this dish with your own two hands, my ducana recipe will set you right.

However, there's an additional reason to learn to make this delicious national dish. For many, making ducana can be something of a rite of passage if you're Antiguan or of West African descent. When you make ducana you carry on a tradition passed on from generation to generation going all the way back to our ancestors who were trafficked from the African continent centuries ago.

When you think of it in this way, learning to make ducana is not only about cooking a delicious meal. It's also about maintaining a link with those around us and passing on our traditions to the next generation as part of our legacy. This is the way I feel about cooking many of our traditional meals, of which ducana is one of the most popular examples.

Making ducana has taught me a few things about life, especially from my perspective as a teacher. Here are my top four.

First, it's not how much you know, but how you make others feel that leaves a deposit in one's life. My former pupils who thank me for what I did for them never talk about the content of my lessons. Instead, they talk about how I made them feel. I believe I was a good teacher, but it turns out that this was not because of how much I knew.

Ducana and saltfish with fried plantains is an ultimate comfort food. It tastes great, of course, with its combination of sweet and savoury flavours, vibrant colours, and varied textures. But it's how it makes you feel that's telling. It's labour intensive, so each meal becomes a labour of love. People who know how much work ducana takes to make, understand what each meal requires. And they appreciate it and you. Never substitute how much you know for how you make people feel.

Second, it's often the small things that count. I continue to be surprised when people meet me and thank me for some small thing I've done for them. I don't usually remember doing it. It was a small thing. I was probably paying forward my debts to those who helped me and my family. It might be small to me but it's often the small things that count. A small thing can make the difference to how something is experienced.

In my ducana recipe below I use green bananas, which is not typical for Antiguan ducana. Through trial and error, I've learned to add it over the years because it adds a little something. Green bananas are high in manganese, potassium, pectin, and vitamin C so they add nutrients to the meal as well as adding flavour. The amount of potassium, for example, is measured in milligrams. But those tiny amounts make a difference. Pay attention to the small things like being kind, being generous, and showing compassion. Often those are the things that count.

Third, don't be afraid of hard work. When you put in hard work you get great results. Ducana is not the easiest of meals to make. It's labour intensive. Just grating the coconuts and sweet potatoes is an effort. But when you've put in the hard work you get a meal that is wonderfully delicious.

It was this perspective that encouraged me to join the teachers strike 45 years ago. It would have been simpler to keep my head down and to not engage. Had I not gone on strike I wouldn't have faced the retaliation of the only teaching job in my local community and the only transfer I had requested in my career taken away from me. But the hard work of going on strike helped to safeguard some of the employment rights of teachers. So never be afraid of hard work. Everything worthwhile takes effort.

Fourth, whatever things of value that we learn in this life must be passed on, or else they die with us. We spend a lifetime learning all sorts of useful things that we wish we'd learned earlier. But so few of us pass it on. That's what this book is about. It's my attempt to pass on some of what I've learned. Ducana is not just about food. Because of its rootedness in our African heritage it's also about passing on a tradition from one generation to another that goes all the way back through enslaved ancestors to our forebears on the continent.

Passing on what we have learned to the next generation is a responsibility which we all share and something that I am passionate about as a teacher. Otherwise, knowledge is lost, and just as importantly, our connections with our ancestors are further diluted. When we pass on what we've learned we enable others to stand on our shoulders and to go further and to achieve greater things than we have so far. It's an investment in the future. In a way we're all called to be teachers and I urge "each one to teach one."

Grandma Mirie's Antiguan Ducana

3 cups grated green banana

3 cups grated potatoes

1 cup flour

1 tsp salt

2 cups milk

2 tsp mix spice

2 tbsp butter

1 cup grated coconut

1½ cups brown sugar

Method:

1. Combine all ingredients

2. Prepare banana leaves by holding over open flame or put in boiling water or use foil lined with parchment paper

3. Put ½ - 1 cup mixture in banana leaves or chosen alternative, fold and secure with string

4. Place in boiling water that covers the ducana and boil for 30-40 mins

5. Remove covering to serve

MIRI-ISM

Bad attitude
is like a flat tyre,
you can't move ahead
until it is changed.
MIRIAM SAMUEL TURNS 90

Journal Prompts

1. Reflect on some advice that had a significant impact on your learning journey.

2. Reflect on a time when hard work paid off and led to a significant achievement. What lessons did you learn?

CHAPTER 4

Grow your garden to multiply knowledge and resilience

Working in the garden stimulates all my senses but beyond that it prepares me for many life challenges and gives me inner peace. I was born in an agrarian community and as long as I can remember, I have always had a relationship with the land.

Raised during World War II on a tiny island, I became acutely aware of the connection between agriculture and food security. As many struggled to feed their families, my mother ensured that we always had an array of crops. She studied the crop seasons to ensure that we were never out of food.

By the age of six, I had my own little plot and ever since I began to know myself, I knew the land. My initial connection to gardening was as a way to produce food for my family. But in my later years, I have embraced it as a way to embody Earth's wisdom. I grew up relying on the *McDonald's Farmer's Almanac* for tips on the best time to plant and harvest. But through years of experience, I have learned how to support my plants through experimentation and observation. Now, both my garden and I are capable of thriving despite adversity.

Over the years, my connection with the land has flourished. I began planting crops like spinach, and eventually graduated to root crops like sweet potato and cassava that can withstand challenging periods of drought. I am also now stewarding my own fruit tree guild in my backyard.

I harvest more produce than I can use so I share these crops with neighbours, friends, or those in need. Growing and sharing nutritious food allows me to make and sustain connections across the wider Antiguan community. One of the things I've learned is this: never hesitate to share your harvest, even during difficult times. Whether I face crop failures or harsh weather, I am committed to sharing because I believe we can always give to each other, because the Earth is so giving to us.

Even better, now that I have become what my granddaughter, Genesis, refers to as a 'wisdom keeper,' I not only share the harvests of my "little ground," with the community, I also share seeds of wisdom from what I have learned and continue to learn. Genesis has inherited my love of the land. We share a passion for nature and we are both students learning from the garden together. She describes it as regenerative learning where we recreate, rebuild, and re-establish life-affirming relationships with nature, the earth, and each other. Nature has the ability to regenerate itself if given the opportunity and we trust the diversity of nature and life itself.

Some may argue that we should simply leave nature to itself. But nature is our origin, our habitat, a whole of which we are a part. It is embedded with our senses, our breath, and our metabolism. We are nature. From the blossoms of the marmey apple trees, I learned the importance of carefully trimming away excess branches and buds from fruit trees to ensure healthy growth and to produce more fruit. I try to bring the concept of pruning to my own life. If you centre your energy in one area, it becomes stronger than if the energy is scattered.

Every day, I focus my intention towards finding my inner strength. Through this practice, I'm able to maintain balance and produce not just an abundance of crops, but agri-products and life lessons for members of my community.

I believe it's this ability to prioritise and focus on what truly matters which allows me to maintain health, happiness, and a sense of fulfilment, just as a pruned tree remains healthy and productive. Plus, I plan to live to be 120 years and to remain healthy on that journey. So, pruning for health and productivity is extremely important to me.

Another gardening lesson stems from a finger rose plant I tended to near a fence. The plant eventually migrated into my neighbour's backyard so I could no longer harvest the plants. One day I approached the finger rose tree from my side of the fence. I whispered to the finger rose plant "You belong to me and it's time for you to give back". Weeks later, the plant grew a branch that extended over my fence. I harvested the finger rose bunch and shared the harvest with the neighbours. I believe that we all come from the earth. Therefore we must always share our harvests with each other.

One of my visions is growing a larger fruit guild for the community. I hope that fruit trees and the tradition of purposeful giving will be a part of my legacy and have a lasting impact on future generations.

In recent times, I have started planting in tyres. Tyre gardens are an eco-friendly way to reuse old tyres and prevent them from ending up in landfills. Recycled tyres make great planters because they are sturdy and withstand heavy wind and rain. They're also deep enough for plants to establish roots, and you can drill holes in them to promote water drainage. As the tyres heat up in the sun, the soil dries faster, preventing root rot. It's also easier to control weed growth in tyre gardens, as the contained environment doesn't allow weeds to spread as easily.

You can set up a tyre garden by filling a used tyre with soil then planting seeds or plants of your preference. Stack the tyres to create raised beds or use single tyres as separate and contained planters.

There is also the social side of gardening that brings me great joy and satisfaction. Nothing beats connecting with a circle of gardener friends and associates. One of the best ways to make the most out of your gardening experience is by joining an informal gardening community or connecting with an organization like Gilbert Agriculture and Rural Development Centre (GARD).

I encourage you to find people who share a passion for gardening and come together to share tips, ideas, and to support each other. From increasing your knowledge and skills to making new friends and connections, a gardening group can help you grow as a gardener and enhance your overall enjoyment of this great hobby.

I have connected with a gardener in Trinidad who has been a source of inspiration. We speak several times a week and share our ideas and experiences. So, whether you're a seasoned pro or a complete beginner, I encourage you to connect with other gardeners either in-person or online to take your gardening to the next level.

As a student of my garden, I've become an advocate of adaptation and abundance. The garden is the foundation of creativity. When we give back, we emulate the spirit of the "giving Earth." Best of all we come from the earth and to the earth we return. So, in about 30 years, even when I am gone, I will still live. I will live through the trees and plants that I have stewarded and the relationships I have cultivated.

For me, gardening is a spiritual experience and will always be a part of my life. There are literally hundreds of references in Scripture to growing and planting – and the book of Genesis begins, with a garden that Adam was supposed to tend. Many of Jesus' illustrations were designed for an agrarian society. These parables presupposed that his hearers would have a frame of reference for planting and growing and tending gardens.

Just like in life, tending a garden brings with it losses and triumphs. Gardening can teach you a lot about life. Here are some tips that I have learned that you can apply to your garden and your life, to reap a harvest that will make you proud.

Appreciate Small Beginnings

Every plant starts with a seed or small shoot. Small beginnings can lead to amazing outcomes in life. Think about the amount of your first pay check from your first job, or how long it took you to read your first book. When you set goals in life, getting started is the hardest part. Starting small is key, and it leads to progress. Your garden may be a few rows of tiny little plants, but soon you will have a basket of home-grown tomatoes or even squash.

What you plant in your mind today will be your harvest tomorrow.

I believe you are what you eat, drink, wear, and think. What you *think* is the soil to your garden. Consider your thoughts. How do you talk to yourself? What you think about you "bring about." You get back what you are giving out. If you are planting negative thoughts in the soil of your mind, then that is what you will harvest in your life.

Stop watering dead plants.

I stopped growing lettuce in my garden because there was too much sunlight and my lettuce wouldn't grow. This is a great life lesson! Stop pouring your focus and energy into things that are not going to grow anymore. Recognize when relationships or priorities are not healthy for you. Pull the weeds that weigh you down.

Find beautiful things between a rock and a hard place.

You have to push through the dirt. We go about our daily business and suddenly *"life"* happens: hardship, disappointments, and struggles. That's like more and more dirt piling on your head. We all have our struggles, but we need to remember - the bigger the trials the sweeter the victory. Push through the dirt into the beautiful sunshine. Be the beauty for others to see.

Death completes the circle of life.

Our society doesn't talk much about death but it's something we will all experience. Plants go through their natural cycle of birth, life, death – repeat. We all have a purpose to fulfil. *Are you nurturing and watering your purpose?* Nothing thrives without consistent hard work and dedication. That includes your garden and your life.

One of the ultimate experiences of gardening is being able to eat what you grow. Fungee and pepperpot is Antigua and Barbuda's national dish. Fungee is made from cornmeal and pepperpot is a thick rich vegetable stew made with an array of vegetables simmered for several hours. Meat is optional.

Whenever I am preparing to make pepperpot, I embrace the spirit of the harvest as I rely on the bounty from my garden. The origins of pepperpot are believed to be West African, brought over by our enslaved ancestors during the transatlantic slave trade. Over time, this recipe has evolved and has been adapted by Antiguans and Barbudans to suit local ingredients and flavours. This "one pot" dish is a symbol of our island's rich agrarian history, melting pot of cultures, and the resilience of our people.

Grandma Mirie's Pepperpot

1 bundle spinach

1 lb eggplant

1 large green papaya

4 small table squash

1 lb peas

1 lb pumpkin

1 lb each ground provisions (sweet potatoes, yams, eddoes)

3 lbs (one lb each) cured meats (salt beef, pig mouth, pig tail)

1 lb chicken (back and neck, drumsticks)

Seasonings to taste

Onions

Garlic

Pepper

Method:

Cut cured meat in small pieces and soak them overnight.

Season the chicken and pre-cook

Boil the meat, peas, beans, and ground provisions until cooked.

Add remaining ingredients and lower heat to a simmer until cooked.

Add seasoning of your choice.

MIRI-ISM

MIRIAM SAMUEL TURNS 90

Soil gives me life. Whatever I desire, I plant it, sow it, give it, and I just sit back in faith to reap my reward.

Journal Prompts

1. Every one's garden is different and so is every one's life. What aspects of your life would you compare to a garden?

2. What are some of the gardening techniques that you can apply to your life during tough times?

3. How do your personal and professional relationships help you grow and navigate adversity effectively?

CHAPTER 5

Transform lives through faith, hope, and hospitality

I remember being confirmed in the Moravian Church by Bishop John E. Knight, when I was a young teenager. But I started attending the Swetes Pilgrim Holiness Church when I was around 17 years and fully committed my life to God. My deep love for God and my unwavering faith began when I was a child. My spiritual journey has shaped who I am to this day.

I didn't grow up in a very religious home, but my love and devotion to God were nurtured by my many church families. I recall going to church several times a week for choir practice, youth service, the standard Sunday morning service, Sunday night service and mid-week service.

Pastor Henry and Sister Rosa Lee had the greatest influence on my young Christian life. I developed a deep friendship with the family which has lasted more than 70 years. I have many fond memories of assisting Sister Lee in taking care of her children, mainly the girls, her first four children. I recall patiently combing the girls' hair, getting them dressed for church, and then hurrying back home to get ready for church. Ironically, over 60 years later, I began combing Sister Lee's hair every week until her death in 2019.

As a young believer, having faith was often challenging. I needed to make some inward changes, since I was spontaneous and precocious by nature. I had to learn to be patient and calm and allow God's will to work in my life. My patience was tested many times throughout my younger years. I wanted to become a nurse and applied to the Government for a nursing position. But I never received a response. To this day, I do not know why I was overlooked. I wholeheartedly believe that becoming a nurse was not what God wanted for me. Instead, God wanted me to become a teacher. This experience taught me patience and to never lose faith.

I found my calling in the church. Whereas many of my friends were active either speaking or singing, I liked being involved in the hospitality aspect of the ministry. Any opportunity to provide a welcoming environment of love, acceptance, comfort, support, and care, for visitors, members, guests, and friends is where I positioned myself.

The art of patience is a quality that I developed in helping with various hospitality roles in the church. Whether it was helping to decorate the church or preparing and serving refreshments, I was often called upon to lead. I am always happy to use my talents and creativity to advance God's kingdom, using the magical hands that I have blessed with and at every opportunity.

One of the most important calls that Christ gives His church is to be welcoming to people. I stood ready to serve people as a way to enhance the worship experience, encourage fellowship and help build a stronger community of believers. We are His ambassadors (2 Cor. 5.20), so Jesus uses us to be His welcoming arms to draw people from the outside into His presence! I believe that a church must welcome not only believers, but also those who may have never been inside of a church.

I have remained a member of the Swetes Wesleyan Church, formerly the Pilgrim Holiness Church, for over 70 years and it remains a solid foundation in my life. I have served as Wesleyan Women's leader, Vacation

Bible School coordinator, Sunday School teacher, and usher. Working alongside my brothers and sisters in the church required patience. Being a part of a team means working with different types of personalities. But through effective communication, good teamwork, and lots of prayer, I can proudly say that I was able to serve in various roles with pride, knowing that I was doing it all for God's glory. It was a faith journey.

During my younger years, I visited various Pilgrim Holiness churches around the island, for open air revival services. I made many lifelong friends through my church community, both in Antigua and Barbados. I also learned many skills within the church that I still rely on today. By being a part of the youth group as well as the choir (even though I can't sing), I learned how to be accountable to those in authority as well as shouldering responsibility as a good team player. I also developed strong leadership and people skills which helped me in my personal development over the years.

Being part of the church community has strengthened my faith in God. I recall with fondness the times I spent at the home of Sarah Gouvia a.k.a. Nen Nen. This kind, caring shopkeeper was an older member of the St. John's Wesleyan Holiness Church, who became a mother figure to me. Whenever we had all-day service at the St. John's church, I would always have lunch at Nen Nen's house, which was on Tanner Street. Nen Nen always welcomed me with open arms and gave me good advice and counsel about life. I would always make sure I carried milk or produce from the garden to show appreciation for her kindness. As I reflect on her generosity, I realise that I have passed on these gifts to many young persons in my church.

I have opened my home and offered many young people refuge from the cares of the world. I also taught many of them how to make some of my recipes, and several of them have gone on to become entrepreneurs using this knowledge. Sowing seeds of kindness is my passion and giving is my love language. I feel closer to God when I am able to help others.

It's amazing how we can use our God-given talents for God's glory. When the Wesleyan Holiness Church started their youth camp in 1973, my husband and I were a part of the Organizing Committee. I helped with the cooking and counselling the young people. It gave me joy to give back to the young people in my church. As I look back at those camp days, I feel blessed, knowing that I had a hand in nurturing and guiding so many of our young people to begin a personal relationship with God.

I look back with fondness at a Sunday School programme that I started in the village of John Hughes, along with three fellow young church members who are no longer with us: Felix Peters, Alice Benjamin, and Beresford Gaynes.

John Hughes is a community dear to my heart since some of my father's family lived there. It was also one of the places the church would visit to host open-air services. I wanted to give back to that community, through its young people, so I encouraged my friends to accompany me to John Hughes on Sunday afternoons.

The loud bass voice of Beresford Gaynes singing well-known hymns attracted the villagers, who sent their children to our Sunday School. After singing a few songs, we would share various bible stories with the youth, and speak to them about giving their lives to God. Many times we had over 20 young people!

This Sunday School continued for many years and continued to grow under the leadership of Rosemarie David (now Robinson). She held Sunday School at the John Hughes School (now *Charlesworth T Samuel Primary School*), for several years.

It's amazing how life comes full circle! I often visit *Charlesworth T Samuel Primary* to give motivational talks to the students and I reminisce about how the Sunday School impacted the community.

I often encounter God in my kitchen and I feel a special closeness and connection when I'm making fudge, jams, jellies, and other confectionery. There's a stirring of emotions mixed with fulfilment, knowing that my culinary creations will bring joy to others. One of my granddaughters once remarked that I always hum while I am stirring the jam or jelly. I was unaware of this, but it's a habit that I probably inherited from my father. I remember him humming various tunes as he toiled in the field.

I enjoy the entire cooking process from start to finish and I equally look forward to venturing out to find all the ingredients for the jams, jellies, and other treats. As I stroll through my garden picking guavas, or when I visit the Davids in Swetes and they give me a bag of plums, my joy begins with the preparation. Our work in the kitchen, or buying groceries, or planning meals reminds us that it is God who feeds us and meets our basic needs. He delights in using us as his "image-bearers" to do his work.

In making jams and jellies, sugar is the main ingredient. When combined with other ingredients, it creates a fusion of tastes and colours. But it must be stirred patiently on low heat to create the highest quality product. The process cannot be rushed. It requires lots of attention. With patience and using the right amount of sugar, in-season fruit, and other ingredients, I have honed the art of creating exceptional jams, jellies, and cheeses (like guava cheese). Just like my faith in God transformed me into the person I am today, so too are my ingredients transformed into tasteful, mouth-watering confectionery.

"Never give up" is a powerful mantra that resonates with me. I liken it to the resilience needed in making fudge or guava cheese and navigating life's challenges, with faith in God at the centre. Here's how I connect the two:

Making fudge requires patience, precision, and perseverance. It's a process that demands careful attention to detail and the willingness to keep going, even when faced with challenges. If you don't pay attention, either the fudge could burn or you could get burned. Keep your eyes on the fudge! Similarly, we must address life's obstacles with determination and a spirit of patience and resilience. This is essential for personal growth.

Just as fudge ingredients must be continuously stirred to achieve the desired consistency, our faith in God is the force that keeps us going during tough times. Believing in His presence and purpose can provide the strength and motivation needed to persevere through challenges — consistent stirring leads to the desired consistency.

The end result of making fudge is a delicious treat that brings joy and satisfaction. Similarly, persevering through difficulties with faith can lead to a deeper relationship with God. The sweet rewards of enduring faith and perseverance can be just as satisfying as enjoying a piece of homemade fudge.

Just as fudge needs to go through processes like boiling and cooling to achieve the right texture, our faith is often tested and tempered through trials and tribulations. Each challenge we overcome with a "never give up" attitude strengthens our resilience and deepens our trust in God's plan for us.

Sharing a batch of homemade fudge with others can spread joy and create lasting memories. Similarly, persevering with faith can inspire those around us and provide hope for future generations. And this legacy is what I want to leave with my ten grandchildren and two great grandchildren – a track record of perseverance despite setbacks. I want to leave a legacy of deep faith in God and be remembered for never giving up, no matter what! My wish for all my grandchildren and great grandchildren is to let faith in God be the guiding force that helps them grow and find sweetness in life's challenges.

A similar analogy can be drawn when I make guava or raspberry jams or mango chutney. These products are preserves made from seasonal fruit. If we preserve fruit in this manner, it can be enjoyed all year round, both in and out of season. If not, the fruit begins to rot in mere days. Preservation leads to sustainability and I often draw parallels with my faith in God and my relationship with Him. Just as jams and jellies preserve the essence of fruit beyond its natural season, our faith and relationship with God can sustain us through various seasons of life, both good and challenging seasons. Here are some specific insights:

Consistency: Just as preserves offer a consistent taste of fruit throughout the year, my faith in God has provided a steady foundation in my life. It remains constant, regardless of the circumstances we face.

Hope: Preserves symbolise hope for the future enjoyment of fruit. In a similar way, my faith in God gives me hope for better days ahead, reassuring me that there is purpose and meaning in every season of life.

Nourishment: Like preserved fruit that provides nourishment even when fresh fruit is scarce, my faith in God has nourished and sustained me spiritually during times of drought or difficulty. It has been a source of strength and comfort to me over the years.

Transformation: The process of making preserves involves transforming fruit into something enduring. Similarly, as I look back on my relationship with God, I see how he has transformed me and has shaped me into better versions of myself even amid challenging circumstances.

Trust: Just as I trust that preserves will keep the flavours of fruit intact, I can trust in God's faithfulness to preserve me through all the seasons of my life. My relationship with Him has deepened my trust and reliance on His unfailing love.

Eating healthy, good-tasting food, and impressing others with our skills, can cloud and diminish the spiritual value of food. Food should point to the Creator and not only the cook. So, enjoy it. Delight in it. See it as God's good gift to you, both as a creator and a consumer. See it as God's kind provision to you, both as the worker and the recipient. God uses us to be his hands and feet. And in our work, we should point to God who sustains us all by the word of his power.

The kitchen is not just a place where food is made. It is a place where God's glory is displayed. This is what faith does. It preserves. My love for God and my culinary talents have served as a source of inspiration, comfort, and joy to those around me.

My faith in God has touched many of the lives of my friends and family. Perhaps in response to the changes they saw in me, all of my siblings have also put their faith and trust in God. My faith and love of God also led me to my life partner, my husband, for 45 years, the Hon. Charlesworth T Samuel. We met as teenagers in church. I recall that I initially gave Charlesworth a hard time when he tried to court me. But his patience and perseverance paid off. Together, our faith and love of God helped us to trust his timing and will for our lives, as we both became teachers, got married, and raised five wonderful children.

I know there are some people who don't have faith. But I confess that I don't know how to do life without faith. When the hard times come (and they will), when disappointments arise, when dreams are shattered, when grief threatens to overwhelm, it is my faith in God that has helped me to keep going. Faith gives me the capacity to face whatever is before me with patience and perseverance. With faith, I never give up.

Grandma Mirie's Fudge

Coconut / Mango - any fruit of your choice

Or Chocolate

<u>Coconut fudge</u>

1 grated coconut

2 tins of milk

2 ½ lb white sugar

1 tsp butter

6 cups water

Method:

1. Add coconut to water
2. Heat for 10-15 mins
3. Strain and add sugar
4. Cook in heavy pot until mixture thickens on low heat and stir to prevent from burning
5. Drop mixture in water, if forms a ball, then remove pot from heat
6. Add butter and beat until creamy
7. Pour in greased container and let cool
8. Cut into desired sized pieces

Grandma Mirie's Jellies

Any fruit (guava, pineapple, raspberries (gooseberries))

Sugar

Water

Method:

1. Boil fruit and strain

2. 2 cups of liquid to 1 cup sugar

3. Cook on high flames until liquid thickens

4. Test - take some in a spoon and pour back in pot if it forms a thread it is ready.

5. Pour in warm jars.

MIRI-ISMS

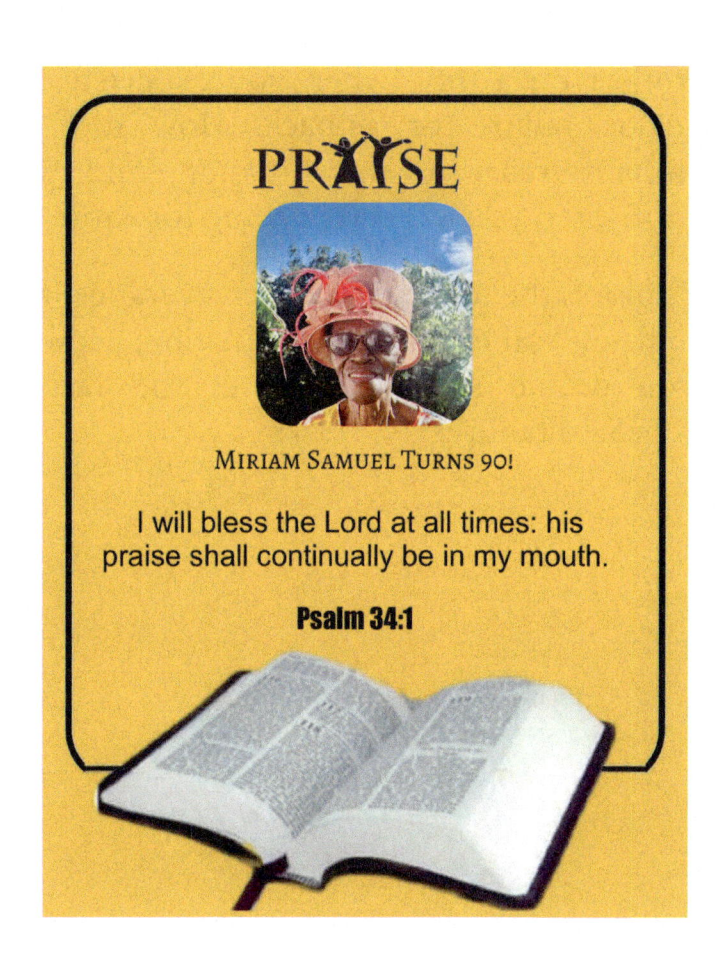

PRAISE

MIRIAM SAMUEL TURNS 90!

I will bless the Lord at all times: his praise shall continually be in my mouth.

Psalm 34:1

Journal Prompts

1. Reflect on a time when you experienced a major failure or setback. How did you initially react to the situation, and what motivated you to keep pushing forward?

2. Explore the concept of perseverance as a journey rather than a destination. How do you define success even in the face of repeated failures?

CHAPTER 6

Generosity – Love to give and give with love

I am fortunate enough to have witnessed the harvest from the seeds of wisdom that have been sown in my life. As I reflect on the countless blessings that have graced my journey of 90 years, there's one quality that stands out and that is generosity. It's a thread that has woven itself into the very fabric of my existence, shaping the way I navigate the world and the relationships I cherish along the way.

From my humble beginnings, I've weathered the storms of life with as much grace and resilience as I could muster. I have discovered generosity as a wonderful quality that can bring joy and happiness to both the giver and receiver. It's the act of giving freely without expecting anything in return, and it can take many forms, from donating time, money, talent and a simple word or gesture of kindness to others.

I was born into a family where hard work was not a choice, but a way of life. Growing up amid scarcity, I learned empathy, the art of gratitude, and the value of a giving heart. My parents, both diligent labourers, imparted the ethos of industriousness and perseverance to their children. Those early years of scarcity sowed the seeds of generosity, instilling in us a profound yet tangible understanding of the struggles that many faced.

Some of my earliest memories of Pa revolve around his generous nature. He was always ready to give whatever he was asked for, often to the chagrin of Ma, who rightfully wanted to ensure her family was prioritised. His willingness to share knew no bounds; he would readily part with anything, even to the extent of giving away a significant portion of the food he tirelessly farmed for our family's sustenance. Ma would sometimes express frustration at his unyielding generosity, but Pa's innate desire to help others remained steadfast. Having little taught us to understand the value of things that many take for granted especially now, in a world where everything can be bought and quickly disposed of.

Marriage brought with it both joy and great responsibility. Alongside my husband, I found myself navigating the delicate balance of raising five children on the modest income earned from our professions as teachers. In a world that often measures success in material wealth, my husband and I measured it in Christian faith, family bonds, and the lessons we imparted to our children.

Our home was filled with items crafted by my hands primarily, because I believe in making the most of whatever you have. From sewing to homemade preserves, cakes, breads, sweets, and drinks, I did my best to make the most of what I had. Each creation was not made only for my family, it was to be shared with neighbours, friends, and even strangers who were in need. Those of us who grew up poor know what it is to need help from time to time. So when you're in a position to be generous, you should do so with a passion. You can never pay back what has been given to you but you can pay it forward.

The fallout from my husband's political career was brutal. I'll say more about this in the final chapter. Our family suffered under the weight of scrutiny, criticism, and the relentless pressure of public expectation. As the spotlight intensified, so did the challenges we faced, from strained relationships to financial instability and hardship. It was a tumultuous time, filled with uncertainty and heartache. Yet, amidst the chaos, we were blessed with acts of kindness that illuminated the darkest of days. Generosity, in its myriad forms, became our guiding light, offering solace and support when we needed it most.

During this time, we were uplifted by the unwavering support of countless individuals, whose kindness manifested through both words and actions. As any mother can attest, the wellbeing of her children becomes the very essence of her purpose, infusing every breath with a profound sense of determination and resilience. Thus, survival transcended mere self-preservation; it became a collective endeavour, shared not only by myself and my husband but by our entire family.

I will never forget the kindness of Ms. Frederick, a shopkeeper from Swetes, a beacon of compassion. She extended a helping hand to my family by providing us with groceries on a weekly basis. Her simple yet profound gesture of kindness not only eased the burden of putting food on the table, but also served as a reminder of the power of community and the importance of looking out for one another. I would never forget the warmth of her smile or the sense of gratitude that washed over me each time we received her gift to us.

Similarly, Richardson's Supermarket, a cornerstone of our economy, demonstrated immense generosity by allowing us to purchase groceries on monthly credit during our time of need. This lifeline provided us with the means to feed our family and maintain a sense of normalcy and dignity amid the upheaval of our lives. The support we received from the Richardson's was not just a financial transaction; it was a lifeline that sustained us during a dark period in our family's life. It was a testament to the power of compassion and community solidarity.

In the face of adversity, these acts of generosity came full circle, reaffirming my belief in the inherent goodness of humanity and the transformative power of compassion. They served as reminders that, even in our darkest moments, there is light to be found in the kindness and generosity of others, and that together, we can weather any storm.

I know and truly understand that we live in a society where we can all find ways to help each other. For me, generosity is a way of life; it shaped my approach to teaching, cooking, faith, and business. It's not just about helping the needy, and it's more than just holding the hand of the weak. To me, it's a chance one gets to give a sense of purpose that manifests in another person's life; it's a chance to help another person hope for a better future. It isn't just about giving material possessions or financial assistance. It's a way of being, a state of heart and mind that compels us to give freely of ourselves – our time, our love, our kindness – without expecting anything in return. And over the decades, this spirit of generosity has been my guiding light, illuminating the path to a life of fulfilment and purpose.

We all have the opportunity to use our talents and skills to serve others. One of the best parts about practising generosity is knowing that your effort is not based on monetary reward, but that your actions will give someone's future a stronger foundation; you can make a difference in someone's life!

I believe in the transformative power of education. Therefore teaching life skills to thousands of children over the course of my career was not only a profession, but also a calling. Despite the meagre financial returns, I did my best to invest myself fully in my students, imparting not just academic lessons but also the values of hard work. Teaching for me extended beyond the classroom, to my family, church, and community. In fact, I've always seen the congregation as an extended family. But church has also been a great place to practise generosity where we give not out of obligation, but out of an innate desire to share the blessings life has bestowed upon us.

Whether supporting fundraisers or lending a helping hand to those in need, a commitment to faith translates into a life of purposeful generosity. I truly believe that one of the secrets to a long and happy life is open-handed generosity. The satisfaction derived from giving, whether in the form of knowledge, handmade creations, or helping out with a task, creates a worthy recipe for living life well!

And speaking of recipes, when I think about generosity in life, I think about one of my favourite dishes, seasoned rice. The truly magical thing about this "one-pot" dish is that you can use whatever you have to make a delicious and satisfying meal. Over the years, this dish has evolved, much like my life, and is a testament to the enduring power of generosity, despite how little you may have.

Why does generosity make me think of seasoned rice? Because seasoned rice whenever I cook it is never just for me and my household. I always cook enough that I can share with friends and extended family. Over the years there are people I know who really enjoy my seasoned rice. So it's a labour of love and I often reflect on the parable about the boy who was selfless in giving his five loaves and two fish to feed the multitude.

So here's what seasoned rice has taught me about generosity and abundance over the years. First, always cook enough for sharing. Be purposefully generous. It shouldn't be an afterthought if you happen to have some leftovers, then you give it away. I usually plan to give most of my seasoned rice away even before I start cooking it.

Second, make varieties of seasoned rice to suit different palates. One of the great things about seasoned rice is that it can have almost any protein in it. Often it has pork, chicken, and beef. But many people don't eat pork. So, whenever I make seasoned rice I make one pot with pork and another without. Because I am seeking to be purposefully generous, when I prepare this meal, I not only suit my preference, but I aim to address the tastes of those with whom I want to share the dish.

Third, I find giving away food is a great way to say I love you. They say that the way to a man's heart is through his stomach. My experience is that this is equally true for men, women, and children. Cooking delicious food for someone, especially when they have no reason to expect it from you, is a great way to express love and kindness.

Fourth, generosity shouldn't be stingy, giving only what we can afford. Generosity at its best must be radical. By this I mean you should give based on what people need and not what you feel you can spare.

And what I've found is this: you can't outgive God. So even when I've given away more than I can afford to give, God gives back to me in good measure, pressed together and running over. In essence, you can't outgive God.

So if you're looking to learn a little about generosity try making some Antiguan seasoned rice from my recipe. Make more than you need. Give much of it away and see what happens.

Grandma Mirie's Seasoned Rice

2 lbs rice

1 lb Peas

2 lbs Cured meat of your choice (salt beef, pig tail etc)

1 lb Chicken (back and neck or drumettes)

1 large Onion

1 head Garlic

1 Sweet pepper

Seasoning to taste

Salt (if needed)

Method:

Cut chicken into small pieces and season.

Cook cured meat until tender. Set aside

Put chicken in a pot without water. Cover and put on low heat to cook.

Add meat, rice, and seasonings with enough water to cook the rice.

Bring to a boil then lower heat or put in the oven at 300F until rice grains are cooked.

Always have hot water on hand if you need to add more water.

MIRI-ISM

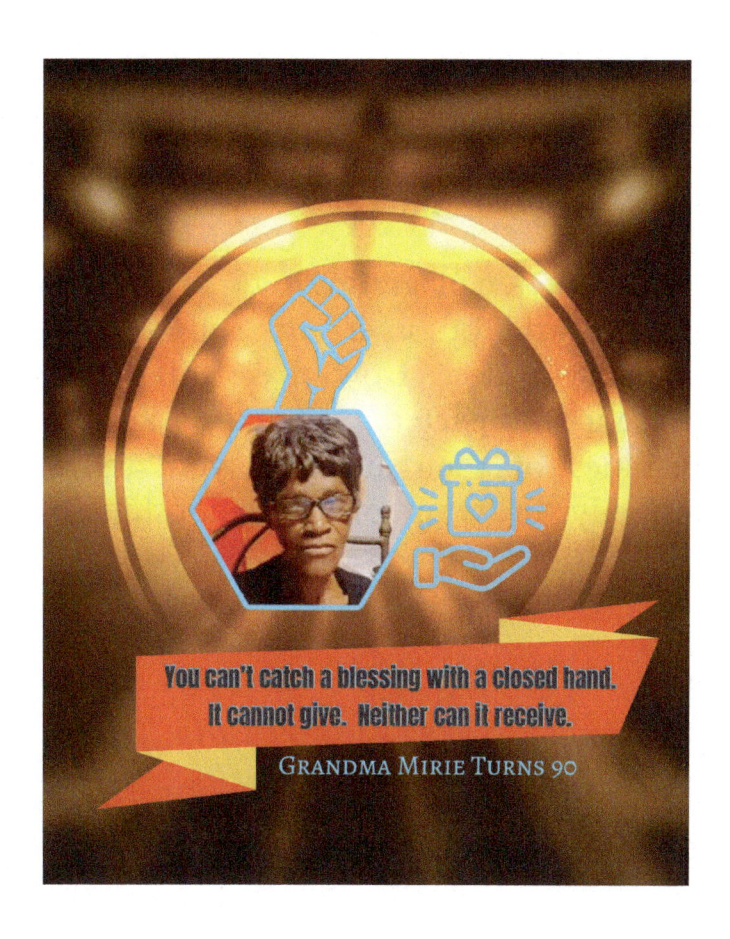

You can't catch a blessing with a closed hand. It cannot give. Neither can it receive.

GRANDMA MIRIE TURNS 90

Journal Prompts

1. Reflect on a time when you showed compassion or kindness to someone. What did you learn about yourself through this act of love towards others?

2. Write a letter of gratitude to someone who has shown you love and support during difficult times. How has this person's presence impacted your life, and what qualities of their love do you aspire to embody in your own relationships with others?

CHAPTER 7

Replenish your mind and keep reinventing your soul

The thrill of discovery fuels my creativity. A friend recently remarked that I am having a spurt of creativity and productivity in my later years. It could be perhaps that I now have more time, freedom, life experience, informal education, and skills training than in my younger years.

"Trying my hand" in anything that is creative, artistic, and related to nature and/or gardening gets me excited. I'm intrigued by originality, and I am always inspired to conceive and or produce something that's unusual. I believe that being rigid, or having an excessive fixation on the routine and obvious can stifle creativity.

I have a penchant for products that can be created by using things made locally and, in particular, things grown in my garden. My love for experimentation, curiosity about learning new things, and steely determination, are elements that I used to lay the foundation for my entrepreneurial endeavours.

I became a full-time entrepreneur in my early 60's, and my daughters affectionately call me a "seniorpreneur". Starting a business at this age came with its challenges, the main ones being my lack of computer skills and the need for financial literacy. I realised that I would have to learn new skills to run a business successfully. So I joined a class to become computer literate. It was a challenge, but I am not someone who backs away from a challenge. I had a hard time understanding all the computer jargon, but I persevered, completed the class, and I now know how to get on to the internet, use WhatsApp, Zoom, and other tools so that I can keep abreast of new developments in my areas of expertise.

With my new computer skills, I was able to develop new products to expand my cooking and baking and channel my creativity in other areas. Initially, my business consisted mainly of baked goods – bread, buns, sweet bread, coconut tart, banana bread, and carrot cake. I sold these goods at many of the supermarkets in the city of St. John's, and even in a few outlets in the countryside.

Around 2015, my granddaughters who had lived with me for a few years relocated to New Jersey and I had more time to devote to my business. I realized it was time to diversify and do things differently. I began to do some internal brainstorming with an element of projection as to what products would appeal to new and existing clients.

Several years earlier, I "tried my hand" with winemaking which I shared with family and close friends. I decided to add wines to my list of products, but I was adamant that all of my wines would be made from local fruit. This was the start of my line of wines featuring over 15 different seasonal fruits including dumbs, guava, mango, raspberry, passion fruit, sorrel, and pineapple.

You can't put new wine in old bottles and as I rolled out my new wines, I had to consider new packaging to be able to sell the wine commercially. I am often told that I am ageing like "fine wine." I quite like this analogy as I have embarked on many new beginnings and ventures later in life that have enhanced my creativity and brought out the best in me. The complexity and depth of flavours in wine develop over time, mirroring the wisdom and richness that come with embracing fresh starts.

The fermentation of wines is an interesting process and is integral to the flavour quality. This is where the fruit changes its structure and blends with the other ingredients to turn into wine. Similarly, change and growth often require time, patience, and transformation. By learning new things later in life, I have embarked on a journey of reinvention, by allowing myself to evolve and adapt to new beginnings over time. Don't be afraid to start over. The next time, you won't be starting from scratch. You'll be starting from experience.

I was also interested in soap-making and bought books, went online, and signed up for classes to learn as much as I could. I now offer a wide range of soaps including charcoal, oats and honey, neem and moringa. I also started making oils from local herbs, and these complement the soaps. My product line offers customers a range of natural products for health and beauty. Currently, I produce over 10 local oils, including lemongrass, neem, moringa, aloe and papaya.

The making of teas was also an easy step for me since I always use local herbs for "bush tea". Tea is the second most consumed beverage after water. I did my own research to learn the art of drying the herbs and then packaging them into tea bags. I now offer over 20 flavours of teas that make enjoyable beverages - hot or cold. The blend of different herbs creates different harmonious flavours. So too, in my life, integrating past experiences, skills and new passions has crafted new experiences and chapters in my life that are uniquely fulfilling and purposeful.

I grew up using many natural remedies from the garden but had limited knowledge of the scientific benefits of herbs like neem, soursop, stinging nettle, and aloe. It was a joy to do the research to learn more about the benefits of herbs I used as a child, and to incorporate them into my products.

The world of wine, soaps and oils is an intricate and complex one. But this part of my work has increased my knowledge of the science behind many herbs. It required me to step out of my comfort zone and learn new and creative ways to develop products after researching the art of winemaking, soap making and oil making.

Without little experience in branding and product development, I once again did the research to launch this new line of non-perishable agri-products — wines, oils, and soap. These new products have a much longer shelf life and I focus on making these products once a month to better manage my time and streamline my business.

There were times when my production of wine, oils, soap, or teas did not come out right, and I had to start over. But each time I had to start a new batch I found that with each misstep, I learned something new. I used these setbacks as opportunities to improve my skills and products.

I am often questioned about new products in the pipeline. I am currently in my "food lab" experimenting with new concepts. Last Christmas, my granddaughter Genesis and I experimented with making sorrel fudge. I'm also working on a new product that will combine my fruit wines and fruit cheeses (guava, mango, pineapple, passion fruit and dumbs) into "boozy" desserts.

I am also looking at ways to honour my family's legacy through my products. It was recently brought to my attention that my siblings and I have been blessed with long lifespans. Except for my older brother Claude, who died at the age of 76 in 2009, my 6 other siblings are alive and well (to the best of my knowledge). Combined, we share a total of over 580 years of Fleming sibling stamina!! This could actually be an island record and an achievement worthy of celebration.

It's a blessing that we still have the rare opportunity of enjoying our golden years together. When we think of ageing it's not about the fine lines but celebrating fine wines. I have thought about how I can create a wine collection to celebrate our shared blessings of long life and good health. A six pack of fruit wines honouring my six siblings is being considered.

In my most creative moments, I often smile benignly at myself, accepting my inevitable foibles, and being realistic about my abilities and limitations. From my early years of finding ways to supplement the family budget, to my current status as a full-fledged entrepreneur, I have always considered myself a survivor. I've developed a good sense of what works and what does not; what I can realistically hope for and what are pipe dreams; I try to determine the difference between what is important and what are distractions. This mindset is essential for guiding the next generation.

I hope that my story will inspire my grandchildren and great grandchildren, and remind them that with good planning, determination and passion, anything is possible, at any age or stage of life. You're never too old to start over!

Grandma Mirie's Soap

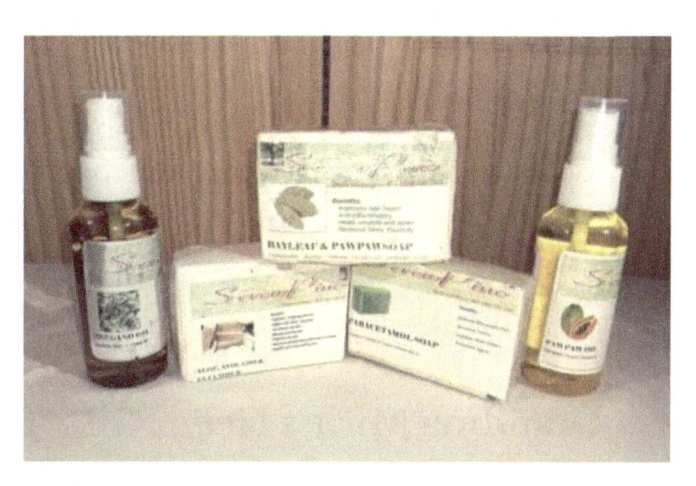

5lb Oil

Lye

Water

Method:

1. Add lye to water (very hot)
2. Heat oil
3. Let lye cool
4. Lye and oil must be between 110-120F

5. Add both and whisk or beat until mixture form a ... when dropped from a spoon it does not sink but stays on top the water.

6. Pour it into moulds

7. Cover with plastic or garbage bags and leave for 24 hours on mould

8. Leave for 3-4 weeks before use

Grandma Mirie's Neem Oil

Base: 12 oz coconut oil

In this case: Neem leaves (dry or green)

Method:

1. Place oil and leaves in container

2. Place container in another container with water over high heat

3. Add hot water at intervals and then let steam for at least 3 hours

4. If leaves are green place over direct heat. Lower heat and let boil until they have dried.

5. Let cool for at least a day, strain and bottle.

Grandma Mirie's Wine

1lb ripe fruit

1 gal boiling water

1 ½ lb sugar

1 tsp yeast

½ lb raisins

Method:

1. Boil water
2. Clean and wash fruits
3. Add boiling water on fruits and leave to cool for 24 hours
4. Add sugar, raisins, yeast
5. Cover and leave for 21 days
6. Strain mixture
7. Let settle for at least 1 week
8. Strain at least 2 times and bottle
9. Seal and label

MIRI-ISM

International Women's Day

90 DAYS

In my day, I wasn't even aware of the glass ceiling
I just focused on working hard.

Had I focused on the glass ceiling,
I would be more focused on my LIMITATIONS
and less on my POSSIBILITIES.

GRANDMA MIRIE'S HERSTORY

Journal Prompts

1. Imagine your ideal vision for a fresh start in an area of your life that excites you. What small steps can you move closer to this vision?

2. Consider individuals who have achieved success later in life after starting over. What inspiration can you draw from their examples to fuel your own journey?

CHAPTER 8

Embrace life with boundless energy and enthusiasm. Adventure awaits!

From time to time, I sit quietly with my thoughts, surrounded by the tangible evidence of my 90 years. I can't help but reflect on the vibrant tapestry of experiences that have woven themselves into the fabric of my life. Born into a world where challenges were as commonplace as the air we breathe, I learned early that each obstacle is an opportunity for growth. My journey as a mother of five and a dedicated wife, teacher and entrepreneur was marked by an unyielding determination to overcome hurdles, instilling in me a resilience that would become the cornerstone of my adventurous spirit.

Honestly, as I grow older, I find myself overwhelmed with gratitude to God for the journey that has brought me to this point – a journey marked by boundless energy, insatiable curiosity, and an unyielding zest for life's adventures. This chapter advocating enthusiasm and adventure encapsulates the spirit that has driven me throughout the decades, propelling me to embrace challenges, learn new skills, and constantly reinvent myself.

From the earliest days of my youth, I've been propelled by an adventurous spirit that knows no bounds. Travelling to Antigua by boat from Anguilla, marked the inception of a transformative journey. It was the first seed planted in the fertile soil of my adventurous spirit. This ignited a curiosity that would blossom into a lifelong love affair with exploration.

As the waves rocked the vessel, carrying my family across the shimmering expanse of the Caribbean Sea, I felt an exhilarating sense of anticipation coursing through my veins. Little did I know that a single voyage would set the stage for countless adventures yet to come, shaping the course of my life in ways I could never have imagined.

Whilst growing up, I found solace and yet excitement in being outdoors, where the earth beneath my feet seemed to whisper secrets of vitality and renewal. Of course, it was easy for my feet to hear these whispers because being barefoot is as natural to me as breathing! They say it's called 'earthing', but I call it life! According to my granddaughter, Genesis, it is also known as 'grounding', a practice that involves connecting directly with the Earth's surface in order to absorb its natural energy. This typically involves walking barefoot on grass, sand, soil, or even concrete, allowing the skin of the feet to come into direct contact with the ground.

Proponents of earthing believe that the Earth's surface is abundant with negatively charged electrons. By making direct contact, electrons can flow into the body, neutralizing free radicals and reducing inflammation. They say it promotes various health benefits, including improved sleep, reduced stress, and enhanced overall well-being. The scientific research on the benefits of earthing is revealing what I already know — gardening is an energetic dance with nature. It fills my days with purpose and joy. There's a profound connection between tending to the soil, coaxing life from seed to bloom, and the boundless energy that courses through my veins. This symbiotic relationship nourishes both my body and soul.

It's a simple yet profound reminder of the interconnectedness of all living things, and the importance of staying connected to the natural world. I've always preferred natural remedies to commercially made products. From herbal teas brewed from plants grown in my own garden to homemade skincare oils and balms crafted from botanical ingredients, nature provides everything we need to nourish and heal our bodies. There's a sense of energy and empowerment that comes from knowing exactly what goes into these remedies. I trust in the wisdom of the earth to provide for our needs as God intended, in the most pure and simple ways possible.

But perhaps the most potent fuel for my adventurous spirit is my willingness to try something new. As a girl Wedged between an older and younger brother, I was extremely competitive and determined to master any skills for which they had an advantage. For example, if my brothers climbed a mango tree, I was determined to do the same. I did not have pants in my wardrobe and wearing a skirt limited my movement. I used my skills in sewing to turn some of my skirts into pants to enhance my agility as a climber. I was always ready for an adventure!

Whether it's mastering a new skill, embarking on a new hobby, or exploring a new corner of the world, I approach each new experience with an open heart and an eager mind. It's this willingness to embrace the unknown, to step outside of my comfort zone and into the vast expanse of possibility, that has enriched my life beyond measure.

As I reflect on my years, the classroom is not confined to the walls of a school; it extends to workshops, community centres, and the boundless expanse of the internet. Yes, the internet has become one of my greatest tools, from social media to videos teaching about everything to be imagined! And don't forget the various hacks. I could watch those videos all day long.

Over the years, every skill that I mastered wasn't merely another feather in my cap; it served as a reminder that curiosity and adventure are ageless companions to a lifelong commitment to learning, growing, and evolving.

A few years ago, vegan cooking became an outlet for culinary exploration and healthier choices, and I mastered the art of crafting delectable, plant-based meals. Over a decade ago, I embarked on a new journey by enrolling in weekly Spanish classes, immersing myself in a world of unfamiliar sounds and vibrant vocabulary. This offered me a fresh adventure and a welcome challenge to my mind and spirit.

My penchant for adventure and maintaining my vitality didn't go unnoticed by those around me. A few years ago, my niece reminded me of my yogurt-making in the 1980's; I almost forgot that little skill. She was only about seven at the time, yet forty years later, she regaled me with details of the yogurt-making machine, tucked away in a corner of my kitchen, covered with a white cloth. She shared that she had been utterly mesmerised by what she perceived as pure magic. She thought that yogurt was bought from the grocery store, not conjured up in the kitchen!

To think that my yogurt-making endeavour left such an impression on a tender mind validates my explorations. Who would have thought that something as simple as homemade yogurt could be such a source of fascination and amusement? I must admit, there is something delightfully mystical about turning a humble jug of warm milk into creamy, tangy yogurt, right in the comfort of your own home.

There is a sense of pride that comes from creating something superior to what can be found commercially. But such is the magical adventure of life – even the most mundane of activities can translate into an extraordinary experience by sparking an adventure in the eyes of a child.

It's worth noting that as an adult, my niece ventured into a highly successful business endeavour, crafting delectable Greek yogurt and healthy treats. You should never underestimate the power of homemade yogurt to captivate and 'culture' the imagination of the next generation! This is a part of the legacy that I want to leave behind. I want to be remembered for unleashing a little bit of magic hidden in every mundane moment if you look at it through the right lens.

Adventure can sometimes be discovered in some of our darkest moments. Sadly my husband passed away in January 2008 and I found myself facing a major crossroad in life. At the age of 73, I made the decision to embark on my first cruise vacation. This journey was about seeing new places and healing. It was also a pivotal moment in embracing profound changes that had shaped my world.

Setting sail to destinations like Alaska and the Mediterranean became more than mere vacations; they were voyages of self-discovery and renewal. I found the vastness of the sea reassuring; reminding me of the endless power of God and the possibilities that lay beyond the horizon. This was the same feeling of adventure that I had experienced as a child on the boat from Anguilla but didn't have the words to express it.

Travelling became a means to reconnect with the adventurous side of me. Along the way, I had the privilege of visiting friends and family in various countries, weaving together the threads of connection that spanned continents and generations. In hindsight, that first vacation cruise marked the beginning of a new chapter in my life. It was truly a testament to my ability to embrace change and to find joy, and even fulfilment in the face of loss. As I continue to seek adventure in my life, I carry the memories of those travels as a reminder of the power of exploration, connection and the vitality that can be found when we fully live our lives.

I encourage everyone to travel and unlock the sense of adventure that can broaden your horizons. All you need is a plan, road map, and the courage to press on to your destination. ("All you need is the plan, the road map, and the courage to press on to ...") As I reflect on countless adventures that have filled my days, I'm reminded of four valuable lessons.

First and foremost, I've learned that true vitality comes from staying connected to nature – from tending to the soil in the garden to feeling the earth beneath my feet. In a world filled with distractions and disconnections, it's essential to nurture this bond with the divine through nature, for it is the wellspring from which all life flows.

Secondly, I've come to understand that the key to a life well-lived lies in embracing the unknown — saying yes to new experiences and opportunities for adventure. It's easy to become complacent, to settle into routines and habits that feel safe and familiar. Fulfilment comes from stepping boldly into the unknown, by opening ourselves to the endless possibilities that lie beyond our comfort zones.

Thirdly, seek knowledge passionately, for it is the key to unlocking the doors of possibility. Be a perpetual student, eager to learn, unafraid of the unknown. The richness and vitality of life is not measured in possessions but in experiences, in the stories etched into your memory and to those you impact and influence over the years, even if you think they are not paying attention.

Lastly, even the most mundane activities hold extraordinary potential if approached with curiosity and creativity. When climbing a tree or riding a bike, embrace a childlike perspective, where every day experiences are avenues for discovery and delight. Look at life through the lens of possibility and appreciate the inherent magic that surrounds us, even in the most ordinary moments.

As I prepare to celebrate my 90th birthday, I do so with a heart full of gratitude for the adventures that have filled my days. With each passing year, my spirit continues to brim with vitality, fuelled by the countless experiences that have shaped my life. And as I continue my journey, I do so with a sense of excitement and anticipation, eager to see where the next adventure will carry me. I promise you that my next series of adventures will not be confined to far-off lands; they will be woven into the fabric of everyday life and filled with vitality.

In recent times, I have embarked on a new food adventure, experimenting with ways to replace wheat-flour-based recipes with gluten-free and Paleo-friendly alternatives. Cassava, with its high resistant starch content, aids weight loss, helps improve gut health, blood sugar and cholesterol levels. I have created a delicious cassava bread, crafted from scratch with ingredients grown in my own garden and nurtured by the warmth of the sun. I am delighted to share this recipe which reminds me of life's simple, yet meaningful adventures.

Grandma Mirie's Cassava Bread

6 large eggs

2 cups cassava flour

1 teaspoon baking powder

1 teaspoon Himalayan pink salt

1 tablespoon honey

½ cup avocado oil or olive oil

½ cup water, room temperature

Beat eggs in a medium mixing bowl. Add honey, oil, and water to the bowl (not necessary to mix).

Add cassava flour, salt, and baking powder to a large mixing bowl. Whisk to mix the dry ingredients together.

Preheat oven to 350 degrees F. Insert a piece of parchment paper into a 9x5" loaf pan, or make sure the pan is well greased.

Slowly add the wet ingredients into the dry ingredients and stir to combine, breaking down larger lumps.

Put the batter into prepared loaf pan and place in preheated oven for 1 hour.

Remove from oven. Carefully remove bread from loaf pan and place on a cooling rack to cool for at least an hour before cutting.

MIRI-ISM

LEAVE FOOTPRINTS OF KINDNESS WHEREVER YOU GO.

Grandma Mirie Turns 90

Journal Prompts

1. Reflect on a time when you felt truly alive and full of energy. What were you doing, and what made that experience so exhilarating for you?

2. Imagine stepping outside of your comfort zone to try something adventurous or unfamiliar. What opportunities for growth and self-discovery await you on the other side of your apprehensions?

Chapter 9

Build a legacy on a foundation of love, lessons, and leadership

It's said that formal learning is like riding a bus: the driver decides where the bus is going; the passengers are along for the ride. Informal learning is like riding a bike: the rider chooses the destination, the speed, and the route. My life has been characterized by many formal and informal lessons. Although I have always enjoyed being the driver, as a wife and mother, I was the front seat passenger, reading the signs, giving directions, and helping to navigate our family's journey.

My husband was first elected to political office in 1976. He was in his thirties at the time and it was a bit of a surprise to us all. He had been very active in local politics and trade unionism all his life but as a researcher and community organizer. Even while he was a university student in Barbados, my husband remained very much involved in Antiguan politics, even returning home in 1971 to support his local constituency campaign in the 1971 general election. This brought to power the Progressive Labour Movement (PLM), a party which we supported. It was this change of government and its promise of a more hopeful future for Antigua that prompted us to uproot the family from Barbados and return home in 1972.

Our family had expanded. Whereas we had arrived in Barbados with three young children aged three and under: Clement, Derede and Megan. We returned with a fourth child, Calvin, born in our "Barbados era." Two years after we returned we had our fifth and final child, Charlesworth Jr.

Upon our return to Antigua my husband was appointed Head Teacher of Jennings Secondary, one of several new secondary schools created under the PLM administration. I was appointed first to the Potters Primary School before enrolling at the Leeward Island Teacher Training Program. I did my teaching practice at St. John's Boy School, now T.N. Kirnon School. After receiving my certification, I was assigned to Pares Secondary to teach Maths and Craft.

In 1974, my husband became President of the Antigua and Barbuda Union of Teachers and served in that capacity until 1976. Life was busy but good. However, it was all about to change.

In gearing up for elections in 1976, the PLM needed to find a new candidate to contest the St Luke's constituency. Their former candidate had crossed the floor to join the opposition Antigua Labour Party (ALP). That MP was from Swetes, the same village in which Charlesworth and I grew up. My husband had gone out on a limb in recommending this candidate to the PLM party leadership and had been involved in the campaign. Charlesworth therefore felt a sense of remorse because of this candidate's defection to join the Opposition Party.

But Charlesworth's support for the campaign and commitment to the Party turned out to be a costly sacrifice for our family. It's not well known that before graduating he had taken some time off from university to travel to Antigua to help with the campaign for the 1971 election. His party, the new formed PLM, won the elections. However, his joy was short lived. He failed his university final exams.

The stress of being an over committed husband, full time university student, part time teacher and volunteer political activist in a different country had overtaken him. Even with the most brilliant and disciplined mind, you can only wear but so many hats. He had overextended himself.

For my husband, failure had never been an option. As a consequence of his academic failure he was faced with two stark choices. Either he would fail to graduate or he could apply to retake his final year. But if he chose the latter he could not continue in the programme of study for which he was originally registered. So he was required to switch his focus away from Mathematics, which was his first love, to Natural Sciences with a specialization in Physics. This is how he ended up with a degree in Natural Sciences rather than in Mathematics, which is what he went to university to study.

At that point I had a VERY frank conversation with my husband in which I told him in no uncertain terms that I required him to step down from everything he was doing, including his part time teaching job, so he could concentrate on ONE thing: rescuing his university studies. This was the dream that I had bought into and I was not going to allow it to become a nightmare. I became the sole breadwinner at that point and found ways to supplement my income. The sale of my crochet hats and bags, Bajan sweetbread and other things became very important at that stage. It was a necessary step to relieve some of the financial stress. Necessity is the mother of invention and I put my skill sets to work to support my family's dream. Charlesworth successfully graduated in 1972 at the age of 33. We returned to life in Antigua with much hope and anticipation.

So can you imagine our horror and outrage when after all the sweat, tears and costly sacrifice, the candidate whose successful election campaign Charlesworth had made significant sacrifices for, crossed the floor to join the opposition ALP? I could feel my husband's disappointment and disgust about this act of betrayal. I was no less outraged.

So fast forward to 1976. PLM is about to seek re-election, but they still don't have a suitable candidate to contest the St Luke's seat who could defeat the incumbent turncoat. Many speculated that Charlesworth Samuel, the headmaster and recent university graduate, would be the ideal candidate to contest the seat. However, my husband assured me and others that he had no interest in running for office. But as nomination day approached, calls for Charlesworth Samuel as a candidate intensified.

One Thursday afternoon while driving home from Swetes after a community craft class, I heard an announcement on a car's loudspeaker. The announcer clearly stated that my husband would be announced as the PLM candidate that very night — in a few hours. I was blindsided!! I felt angry, shocked, betrayed, and scared. This move meant that as a civil servant he had to resign his role as Head Teacher and suddenly my role would change too. I would cease being the wife of a Head Teacher, a role that I had assumed 10 years prior, and was very comfortable with, to become the wife of an MP. I was outraged because I believed that the life changing nature of this move required deep discussion and thoughtful planning.

But like any supportive wife in my role as the front seat passenger, I put my disappointment behind me and stood ready to support my husband's dream. Two hours after hearing the shocking announcement, my children and I got dressed and we were presented as the wife and family of Charlesworth Samuel, PLM candidate for St. Luke.

The election was literally two months away. We joined the campaign trail, a path that I had never considered. But what happened next was in many ways disastrous and in other ways deeply fortunate. My husband was resoundingly elected as MP of the St Luke's constituency. However, his party, despite winning the majority of votes, did not win the majority of seats. So rather than entering parliament as a member of the government as was widely expected, he entered as a member of the opposition. He was to remain in opposition for the next 28 years. He stood for office in 7 elections with three different iterations of his party: PLM, United National Democratic Party (UNDP) and the United Progressive Party (UPP), as well as standing as an independent candidate.

In the 1970s Members of Parliament weren't paid well. Opposition MPs were paid even less and overnight, my husband's salary decreased by more than 60 per cent. This sparked financial chaos in our household. The outcome of the 1976 election was a disaster for us economically, socially, and emotionally. My husband had given up his very successful role as principal in order to run for office and we were facing an outcome that neither of us had expected, with disastrous financial consequences.

It was at that point that we had to decide what we would do to secure our future. For Charlesworth, he decided that he needed to become self-employed and began distance learning to become a lawyer. It would take him the next 15 years before he qualified because he was doing this while serving as an MP, a teacher in a private school, and father to 5 children, all who needed his guidance and instruction. For my part, I once again turned to informal learning and entrepreneurship and used my talents in craft and baking to make and sell goods to supplement our now less than modest salaries.

Lifelong learning was embraced in our house. One of my sons says that one of his earliest memories of his father is waking up in the middle of the night to go to the bathroom and seeing his father studying, while everyone else was asleep. This was partly because it was one of the few quiet moments in a household of five children. In addition, his new life as an MP was extremely demanding as he had to spend a significant amount of time in the constituency.

Our children witnessed first-hand the sacrifices of lifelong learning, as my husband studied to become a lawyer. I too had a lot to learn. I had to become a better money manager and find ways to supplement our income to help make ends meet. Our life was one of struggle and sacrifice and for the next few years I supported my husband as he fought hard on the political scene. Throughout this challenging period we ensured that we created a loving and nurturing environment for our children. I learned that little is much if God is in it. This experience also strengthened my faith as a Christian and once my children were happy, I found the confidence and strength to press on.

After 28 years in opposition, our political party, now called the UPP after a series of mergers with other parties, won the 2004 elections. After seven consecutive elections Charlesworth was finally in government and was appointed Minister for Agriculture, Lands and Marine Resources. I would have a new role too. I would now cease being wife of an opposition MP, to become wife of a government minister. Life was changing again. But I was ready to support the dream.

A few weeks after the 2004 election victory, two of our children, Clement and Megan, shared the exciting news that they had both been offered places to study for the Bar in the UK. It was a proud moment for me, as both were pursuing law as a second career. Clement is also a Telecommunications Engineer, and Megan is a Chartered Accountant. Their achievements resonated deeply with me, as they exemplified the principle that my husband and I had always preached – "Never Stop Learning."

Like their father nearly twenty-five years earlier, because of family and work responsibilities, becoming law students would require sacrifices. They had continued full time employment and with young families had carved out time so they could study law through a distance learning program. This approach allowed them to complete their Bachelor of Laws degree (LLB). However, if they wanted to practise as lawyers, they would have to be accepted to the Bar and this required graduation from an accredited Bar Vocational Course. All such courses required law students to study on site.

Both Clement and Megan faced challenges in accepting their places to study for the Bar because they needed a plan for childcare during their studies. I immediately volunteered to accompany them to Wales to support them in pursuing their dream. I was determined to do my part to ensure that they succeeded, even in the face of obstacles to lifelong learning. After all, this is a road that I had travelled before as a way maker and dream supporter for my family.

This would be my third journey to a new country to support the dreams of my loved ones. The experience of supporting my children as they pursued their dreams of studying for the Bar in the UK was a profound embodiment of my own commitment to lifelong learning.

My first journey, recorded in Chapter 1, occurred when I was a young child, moving with my family from Anguilla to Antigua in pursuit of my parents' dream of a better life. My second, recorded in Chapter 2, was as a wife and mother to young children moving from Antigua to Barbados in support of my husband's and my own dreams of a better life. This next move would be my third, to Wales as a grandmother to young children in support of two of my adult children's dreams of a second career.

As a former teacher I understand that lifelong learning encompasses not only formal education but also the continuous pursuit of knowledge, experiences, and personal growth. By supporting my children in the pursuit of their dreams, I was actively engaging in the principle of "Never Stop Learning" in a deeply meaningful way.

Accompanying Clement, Megan, and our grandchildren to Cardiff for a year was a decision that I made wholeheartedly. I also made the decision to bring my granddaughter Tiffany along, as I wanted to ensure that the entire family could share in this enriching experience. So seven of us, including Clement with his daughter Lindsay, Megan with her sons Noah and Aron, Tiffany, and myself, embarked on this transformative journey to ensure that Clement and Megan could pursue their dreams, with the peace of mind of having their young children by their side.

The year spent in Cardiff was nothing short of extraordinary, and the impact it had on all of us was profound. The challenges, the triumphs, and the depth of learning that occurred during our time there were truly remarkable. As a retiree, I found a circle of like-minded individuals and made lifelong friends. I immersed myself in an unfamiliar culture with new customs, foods, and way of life. This experience not only strengthened our family bonds but also provided invaluable lessons and insights that enriched our lives in ways that extended far beyond the realm of formal education.

The experiences we shared in Cardiff deserve a chapter of its own. It was one of the richest periods in my life. The support we received from the community and church was warm, deep, and unrestrained. The grandchildren all flourished in their new schools. My son, Calvin, had been living in the UK for over a decade, so he and his family travelled to Cardiff regularly and we travelled to London to visit his family.

I had previously made several trips to the UK over the years and had spent my long leave before retirement as a teacher, between the UK and Canada. So I had established an existing network of friends and relatives there. So my year in the UK enabled me to reconnect with a circle of family and friends I had developed over many years.

What made that period so rich was that we were all learning together. My adult children were enrolled in a formal course of study which was not only academic, they were also learning how to embody the identity of becoming members of the Bar. My grandchildren were, of course, learning in school, but they were also learning how to adapt to a new culture among people of unfamiliar accents and to weather in Cardiff very different from the Caribbean. Additionally, Megan's husband Hendy was accepted into an MBA course in Cardiff only a few months after she started her BVC studies. So he too soon joined our learning community which spanned three generations.

As I reflect on this period and how our learning community evolved, it brings to mind one of my products, kombucha, and its continuous fermentation process and healing properties. Kombucha has its origins in Japanese culture over 2500 years ago and serves as a powerful metaphor for lifelong learning.

The SCOBY, or symbiotic culture of bacteria and yeast, is the heart of kombucha, transforming sweet tea into a tangy, effervescent beverage through the process of fermentation. Just as kombucha undergoes an ongoing transformation through fermentation, our lives can be a continuous journey of growth and development. Much like tending to a batch of kombucha, lifelong learning requires dedication, patience, and a willingness to adapt to new circumstances.

In fact, learning to brew kombucha is part of my own lifelong learning. A few years ago, I'd never even heard of kombucha. But through my grandchildren, I was attracted by the potential health benefits that it offers. And then, of course, I began to experiment with making my own blend. Later in the book you can find my recipe for kombucha.

In the process of brewing kombucha, we must monitor the fermentation, make adjustments, and learn from the outcomes to refine our craft. Similarly, in life, we encounter new experiences, challenges, and opportunities that shape us and require us to adapt and learn. Continuous fermentation reflects the idea that knowledge and personal development are not static but rather dynamic and ever evolving.

Furthermore, just as different flavours and variations of kombucha can emerge during the fermentation process, lifelong learning exposes us to a diverse array of knowledge, perspectives, and skills. This parallels the concept of being open to new ideas, experiences, and mindsets.

Moreover, the patience and attentiveness required to maintain a healthy fermentation process mirror the qualities needed for effective lifelong learning. Both endeavours demand a willingness to observe, reflect, and adapt over time. I have come to appreciate that both processes are not merely about reaching a final product or a specific goal. It is about the quality of the journey, the lessons learned along the way, and the personal growth that results from the experience.

People sometimes ask me the secret to ageing slowly. This is definitely one of them: Keep your mind and body active. And one of the best ways to keep our minds active is to remain curious and never stop learning.

Grandma Mirie's Kombucha

- 1 SCOBY (symbiotic culture of bacteria and yeast)
- 1 cup of starter tea (previously brewed kombucha)
- 4 black tea bags
- 1 cup of sugar

- Water

- Glass jar

- Cloth or paper towel

- Rubber band

Instructions:

1. Boil 4 cups of water in a pot. Once boiling, remove from heat and add the tea bags and sugar. Stir until the sugar dissolves, then let the tea steep for about 10-15 minutes.

2. Remove the tea bags and let the sweetened tea cool to room temperature. It's important that the tea is not hot when you add the SCOBY, as high temperatures can harm it.

3. Once the tea has cooled, pour it into your glass jar. Add the starter tea and place the SCOBY on top.

4. Cover the jar with a cloth or paper towel and secure it with a rubber band. This will allow the kombucha to breathe while keeping out bugs and debris.

5. Store the jar in a warm, dark place, away from direct sunlight. Let it ferment for 7-10 days, depending on your taste preference. The longer it ferments, the more tangy it will become.

6. After the fermentation period, taste the kombucha. If it's to your liking, you can bottle it. If you want it to be more carbonated, you can do a second fermentation in sealed bottles for a few days.

7. Store the bottled kombucha in the refrigerator to slow down fermentation and enjoy it cold.

Remember to save some of the kombucha from this batch to use as starter tea for your next batch. Enjoy your homemade kombucha!

MIRI-ISM

"Knowledge is a garden.
If it isn't cultivated, you
can't harvest it."
— African proverb

Celebration of Life

Journal Prompts

1. What new areas of interest have you been curious about exploring? How can you cultivate a mindset of continuous learning and self-improvement?

2. How can actively listening to and learning from those who hold differing viewpoints enrich your understanding of the world?

FINAL WORD
By Calvin T Samuel

Serving Instructions for Rhymes in Her-story

Mark Twain is famously credited with the saying: "History doesn't repeat itself, but it often rhymes." (We now know that Twain almost certainly didn't say this but it remains a profoundly wise saying, whatever its origins).

Put more simply, history certainly does NOT repeat itself. Yesterday is in the past and remains forever beyond our reach. Tomorrow is not guaranteed. We only have today, which makes each new day a treasured gift.

Nonetheless, elements of the present, though they aren't repetitions of the past, certainly have resonances with what has gone before. However, we can only recognise patterns between the present and the past if we have some awareness of the past.

In many ways, this is partly why we pay attention to history and today's technology has enabled us to be more effective in recording past events and experiences to make historical comparisons and create a more accurate perspective.

If we're sufficiently attuned to the rhymes and cadences of yesterday, we might just have a better chance of understanding today, and better recognise trends which can help shape our tomorrows.

The philosopher George Santayana argued: "Those who cannot remember the past are condemned to repeat it" (*The Life of Reason*, 1905). Winston Churchill made this saying much more widely known by quoting Santayana in a 1948 speech to the British House of Commons: "Those that fail to learn from history are doomed to repeat it." Churchill's perspective on the utility of history is "the longer you can look back, the farther you can look forward."

Churchill himself was one who learned from history. The point at which he quoted Santayana in his 1948 speech, he was still smarting from his humiliating election defeat in 1945, only mere months after leading Britain and the Allies to victory at the end of the second world war. But he went on to lead his party to a second successive electoral defeat in the 1950 elections, at nearly 77 years of age. Churchill remains the only person to win a parliamentary majority for a second non-consecutive term as British Prime Minister after suffering electoral defeat.

Grandma Mirie grew up in a British colony under the governance of Churchill. It is not clear how much of his philosophy she was exposed to during her formative years, but she too has certainly embraced the relevance of history in shaping the future. Moreover, she has also embodied his preserving spirit and self-confidence.

So follow her-story and delve further into the past than merely the news of last week, last year or events of the last decade, to learn invaluable lessons applicable to the present which will give you foresight of the future. Simply put, listen for the rhymes of history. You can 'learn vicariously and by analogy to avoid stumbling in the missteps of those that came before you, for this is the humblest of acts.' ("Why You Must Study History, Now More than Ever Before," *Medium,* July 2019).

This is what this book represents. It's an invitation to listen to the rhymes of history by engaging with the stories of one who has lived long and deep, who has been listening to the rhymes from her-story.

In Miriam's own story we might notice multiple occasions when history rhymes. For example, across the book we hear of her three life-changing journeys to live in another country. Her first as a young child, her second, as a mother to young children, and her third as a grandmother tending her grandchildren.

In her empathetic approach to teaching and her sensitivity to children from economically disadvantaged backgrounds, we might also notice the rhymes with her own humble upbringing. This meant that she was well positioned to be a role model and advocate for the children of the less fortunate.

Miriam's courage and creativity in setting up a business after retirement when many others might have been inclined to seek out a quiet life, is another instance when history rhymes. She was open to taking the risks of a new venture, at least in part, because she had been in a front row seat observing her parents taking the risk of starting over in a new country. Moreover, she was willing to shut this business down in order to go off to Wales to support two of her children in their law studies. Once their studies were complete, she later set up a second business, *Screw Pine,* with a new line of products.

Her-story is a perspective shaped from reflections on 9 decades of invaluable lessons. Her recipes too, passed down through the generations undergoing continuous improve‐ment, carry explicit resonances with past history. There's no need for you to figure out on your own through trial and error how to make seasoned rice or ducana. This book offers you a recipe and a cultural reference that has been tried and tested. This enables you to draw upon the expertise and wisdom of those who've gone before you.

And in a very real sense that's what this book is all about. It offers recipes for life from someone who has lived long and deep in the hope that by looking back at her life we might hear some resonances in our own lives.

So, this is not a book to be read swiftly. Instead, read it slowly and reflectively, pausing often to listen for the resonances when history rhymes. And when something of Miriam's history does indeed rhyme with your experience, note it, learn it, and absorb in a few hours, what it took her decades to learn. Then find ways to pass it on to those who come behind you. The prompts at the end of each chapter are designed to evoke self-reflection and discussion about your own legacy. You may find yourself reading and re-reading.

The legacy that Miriam wishes to leave to those who come behind is not to be measured primarily in money or assets. Rather, it's to be measured in fulfilment, joy, generosity, and a sense of purpose. The opportunity to develop a spark and the subsequent fire that drives creative people to new and greater achievements later in life is only enjoyed by a few. We are grateful that she has the experience, drive, cognitive skills, and self-confidence to continue to pursue her dreams.

So, live your life with purpose and generosity of spirit. Love your friends and foes. Continue to grow. Be rich in spirit! Be open to adventure and never stop learning.

As the family chaplain, I offer these words of wisdom that we have derived from Grandma Mirie's life. On behalf of my family, may you focus on:

LOVING Being passionate about what you do and the people around you.

LEADING Turning dreams ideas and ambition into action through continuous learning.

LEGACY Sharing your expertise, knowledge, and experiences to help future generations make more informed decisions. Leave behind an inheritance that money can't buy.

Rhyming Recipe

A recipe expressed in the form of a rhyming poem. This was a common expedient for homemakers to memorize recipes in the late 19th and early 20th century.

In a garden of dreams, where faith meets joy,
Two loving hands and a heart so coy.
Entrepreneurial spirit, adventurous soul,
Kindness and generosity, the ultimate goal.
Mix in some laughter, a dash of belief,
Sprinkle in confidence, the magic relief.
Her recipes are treasures, a legacy so rare,
Bread warm as hugs, fudge beyond compare.

Jams and jellies, sweet with care,

Teas to soothe, oils beyond compare.

Wines that sparkle, kombucha divine,

Each sip a memory, in the vineyard of time.

Her love blooms like flowers, in the sun's warm embrace,

Her spirit shines brightly, leaving a trace.

Of all she has given, of all she has done,

Her legacy lives on, like the setting sun.

Cheers to our mother, at ninety so grand,

A true inspiration, across the land.

May her recipes and characteristics blend,

In this book of loving and leading that will never end.

- The Samuel Clan

Acknowledgments

I'm grateful to my co-authors Clement Samuel, Derede Whitlock, Megan Samuel–Fields, Calvin T Samuel, Lisa Francis–Peters, and Genesis Whitlock. Thanks to Tiffany Samuel, Tiana Dinard-Samuel, Fletcher Dinard-Samuel, and Inger Jarvis, who were contributors. Special thanks to Odessa Whitlock for her painting that has been adapted as the cover of the book.

About the Author

As a veteran teacher, I have always been a lifelong hands-on learner. Growing up in the post World War II era, food shortage was the norm and I learned to cook at an early age, using an array of creative ingredients as a way of survival.

I discovered my love for baking as a teenager, during my Home Economics Class. As a young wife and mother with a growing family, there was no bakery in my village and it was more economical and convenient to bake my own bread. This became a favourite pastime and my passion for baking grew from bread to cakes, which I happily shared with friends and family.

In the Caribbean, nothing says home, like the smell of baking and when I turned 50, I started to make plans to create a nest egg for retirement. I opened my bakery at my home in 1985 and cultivated a small client base. By the time I retired in 1994, I had expanded the bakery and invested in a plant with commercial equipment to steadily grow my business.

For the past 30 years, I have supplied several supermarkets and small shops in Antigua and Barbuda with fresh supplies of baked goods. Although baking can be quite labour intensive, I find it relaxing and rewarding. As long as you love to bake, life is bound to be sweet.

I am also an avid gardener and grow a variety of crops in my backyard. My small business called *Screw Pine*, has expanded beyond baked goods. I use fresh produce from my garden as the main ingredients in over 90 agri-products. These include wines, oils, teas, jams, jellies, and local confectionery.

I wear many hats but I am most proud of my role as mother and grandmother. This book is a tribute to all mothers—the silent heroes, the guiding lights, the eternal pillars of strength.

Printed in Great Britain
by Amazon